A LITTLE BIT
OF EVERYTHING

Northampton Heritage Hunters

www.northamptonheritagehunters.co.uk

A LITTLE BIT OF EVERYTHING

ISBN 978-0-9521997-3-1

First Published June 2009
by Northampton Heritage Hunters

Printed in Great Britain by
www.direct-pod.com

A LITTLE BIT
OF EVERYTHING

INTRODUCTION

A Little Bit of Everything is produced by the Northampton Heritage Hunters history group. Northampton Heritage Hunters was formed in 2006 and its members are all amateur, but enthusiastic, history seekers. A grant was obtained from the Heritage Lottery Fund to enable us to publish our stories, either remembered in our weekly musings, or researched for a broader view. Our interests are varied and cover a wide range of subjects. Our aim was to show Northampton and some of its people through our eyes and to touch on some of the characters that have graced our town, whilst also showing how the town has changed since we were young.

A wit once said that 'nostalgia is a thing of the past'. It is hoped you will enjoy this book in the reading as much as we did in the writings.

Northampton Heritage Hunters

CONTENTS

Chapter 1
EARLY MEMORIES

KINGSTHORPE HOLLOW, NORTHAMPTON

Kingsthorpe Hollow was a very busy thoroughfare, always busy with boot and shoe workers hurrying to and fro from the various shoe factories sited there and also because it was on the main bus route to Northampton town centre and Kingsthorpe. The bus stops were a place where you met friends and neighbours, a place where you heard the latest gossip and news of the area. People always seemed pleased to see you, as were most of the bus conductors who, being regular on the routes, became very familiar faces. There always seemed to be a queue at the bus stop, by the time the buses reached the 'Hollow' from Kingsthorpe they were often full, especially in the rush hour, so folk had to wait for quite some time, although buses ran very frequently then.

My best friend Ann Stonebanks lived in Monarch Road, so a great deal of my time was spent down the 'Hollow'.

My friend's mother was widowed during the 2nd World War when Ann was 6 months old, so unfortunately never knew her father. Her mother always seemed to be working, her house shone, she was a very kind, private person with a good sense of humour. Mrs Stonebanks worked for Lewis's, a shoe factory in St James's area. She, like most women working in the shoe factories, would leave her work to hurry home each morning to provide a midday meal for her family, nearly all workers in the factories would go home for a hot meal at this time and then hurry back to work for the afternoon session, this was a time when strict time control was enforced with clocking in machines used morning and afternoons. Often the bosses were sympathetic towards these women and would often turn a blind eye to those returning a few minutes late. Public transport was the only means of travelling to work if you were not fortunate enough to live near your employment.

Mrs Stonebanks always boasted that she had never been drunk in her life, that was until my 21st birthday, when my

 father finding that he had run out of drink introduced his own made wine, we have a photo of her looking very happy, and wearing a very crooked hat.

Mrs Stonebanks without her hat at my 21st birthday

I remember calling in for Ann on Saturday mornings on the way to the ABC cinema which held a children's Saturday morning club and see her mother bending over her kitchen sink using a wash board whilst boiling her washing in a boiler, with mangle, blue bags and starch at hand, her house full of steam. Ann always had the whitest school blouses imaginable despite being known at school as 'Inky Stonebanks' - she always ended the school day covered in blue ink.

We went roller-skating and rode our bikes speeding over the ramps in Barratts Shoe Factory yard opposite her house, I can't remember any cars ever being parked there, but there were plenty of cycles. We bought our first packet of Woodbines from the corner shop in Monarch Road and went to Ann's house to smoke these cigarettes and to play with our hoola hoops whilst listening to her Buddy Holly records. When Ann's mother came home she said, 'who's been smoking?' of course we played the innocents.

The parade of shops in the Hollow stocked everything imaginable. There was Margaret's the haberdashers who sold everything from buttons to clothing, Archers fish and chip

shop, where the queue on a Friday evening stretched for yards along the pavement. There were butchers, chemists, greengrocers and a bakery. Maureen's the hairdresser, Stoughton's the animal feed and seed shop, Robinson's the building suppliers, to name a few, but of most interest to us was the cinema called the Coliseum. This building was known as the flea pit, I always covered my head when I went there to prevent catching fleas, inside it was so dark, the lone usherette, who also became the ice cream seller during the interval, used to guide people to their seats with a small torch and if anyone was talking would shout 'shut yer gob.' I remember the seats being very rough and itchy and of course the air was thick with cigarette smoke. Sometimes, if it was a film that we really liked we would stay from thebeginning of the matinee and see the film several times over, there was no record of when you came in, and the film just kept rolling until the cinema closed for the night, except for the frequent times the film reel broke and then chaos broke out with people shouting 'put a penny in' and stamping their feet.

Another place of interest as we grew older was The Cabin, this was a Teddy boy café. We would walk past feeling very brave as Teddy Boys had a bad reputation, supposedly carrying flick knives and bicycle chains, but actually they were really nice boys who loved rock and roll music, wore draped jackets, drainpipe trousers, crepe soled shoes, shoe string ties and had DA (duck's arse) haircuts. This was in the late fifties, when most men wore sombre suits and white shirts. It also was the beginning of the liberation in fashion and youth, with loud rock and roll music, the start of cafés as meeting places, Wimpy Bars selling frothy coffee, American fries, and Coca Cola, very exciting to the young, but not so to many of the older generation who found this change in society very difficult to understand.

When I pass through Kingsthorpe Hollow now it feels so impersonal, very few pedestrians walk the pavements, few shops remain, no real landmarks are left apart from the shell of Barratt's Boot and Shoe Factory and blunt dark flats have replaced the terraced houses.

Whilst at school I remember a teacher asking Ann where she lived, when she replied Kingsthorpe Hollow, the teacher said, 'it sounds like a fairy glen,' perhaps she wasn't too wrong, as to us it was somewhere very special.

Polly Allom 2007

THE MOUNTS, NORTHAMPTON
around the 1950s

As we lived in St.Michaels Road the Mounts area featured quite a lot in my young life. My school was St.Marys Catholic School whose grounds backed onto the Notre Dame. My very first Teacher was Sister Austin and we had regular visits from a very popular Father Galpin who was probably involved more with the children from Nazareth House. This was a children's home adjacent to the Cathedral on the Barrack Road, these children walked daily from there in a 'crocodile' to St.Marys.

There was always a Police constable stationed outside to see us across the road four times a day.

One of my classmates was immortalised to me when we were asked to do some fancy artwork with our initials – hers were SoD, Sheila O'Doherty.

The Social Services building now stands where my school used to.

Saturdays were highlighted by the morning picture show for children at the ABC cinema. We were known as ABC Minors and sang a rousing song. Here for a few pence we could be transported into a fantasy world, there was no T.V. so this was our entertainment. The manager, known to us as 'Uncle Len', owned two Alsatian dogs and as a birthday treat members were called on stage and allowed to shake a paw. Here I rose to the dizzy heights of an ABC monitor, which in reality meant I was responsible for keeping children quiet and cleaning up after they had gone home.

On Sundays I would go with my Dad to pay for the newspapers to a little newsagents shop quite near 'the top' of

Lady's Lane and once a month he would buy a large box of Cadburys chocolates for Mum, or if money was a bit short then it would be a smaller version.

Our shoes were mended by a Cobbler on the corner of the Mounts and Lady's Lane when funds were available, otherwise Dad would put stick-on soles on to make shoes last longer.

Another Sunday ritual, probably during and just after the war years, was for Dad to take the joint and batter mixture, covered with a tea towel, and carried very carefully from home to a baker for cooking. I don't remember exactly, but it was either in Gt.Russell Street or Earl Street. Dad would call into the Trades Club, then in Overstone Road, for a pint (or two) until the appointed time for collection of our roast beef and Yorkshire pudding.

Earl Street had a very good Chinese laundry, which did a roaring trade long before the launderettes took over, as no one had washing machines. Our cotton sheets and pillowcases were returned starched and very white in a brown paper parcel.

On the corner was Claude Jones, the jewellers' shop with interesting items to view. The second-hand section was often goods that had been pawned. When owners didn't, or couldn't, redeem them, then the family treasures were sold.

Once I started work and had a little money to spend on a luxury item, my choice was the hairdressers. Mum had been going for years to one on the Mounts. A lady called Vera owned this; in the main she only had one junior helper so it was a case of being patient until Vera could get around to you. She was very good in that she opened until very late at night, which meant we could go after work, with all the waiting around I can remember getting home at 9.30pm! This was just for a cut, wash and set as it was then, hair was wound round rollers and then you were handed a magazine and left to dry under a huge drier that looked like a space machine.

A 'perm' was a different matter altogether, this had to be on a Saturday as it was a lengthy process. You would wait to have your hair washed by the junior, then wait again until Vera got to a stage where she could leave her present customer, many times hair had almost dried, but she carried on. Perm solution was applied and then hair wrapped in paper and clamped with something that looked like a large bulldog clip attached to a wire. By the time the whole head had been clamped you had sunk at least 3 inches into you chair with the weight and the whole thing looked (and felt) like medieval torture. The end result could be a bit dicey too, too little time for it to work and the hair was still straight or too much and you ended up with a mass of frizz.

When it was right you came out of there feeling glamorous, as well as light-headed. This whole process could keep you on the premises for around four hours, but the entertainment for me was watching the owner work. She was a heavy smoker and over the years had developed a technique with a cigarette the, likes of it never seen before or since. She could have a lighted cigarette in her mouth, smoke it, talk and work (moving around too) and the ash would get longer and longer until all she had left was ash and the tip. Sometimes it would curl and I would sit watching absolutely fascinated waiting for it to fall, in all my time there I never once saw that happen, was she the original 'fag-ash Lil'?

J.M.Clements 2007

An excerpt from Betty Mallard's (nee Waterfield) story

Roughly a period 1942 – 47 in Green Street, Northampton

One night I was woken by a rat tatting sound, Billy had also woken up, we hung our heads out of the window as the noise got louder. We saw to our horror a plane going down to crash nearby. The rat tatting noise was the bullets going off in the heat, the plane was just a ball of fire, it landed in Gold Street and it was such a mess. Mum had seen it too, coming towards her as she lay in bed; it was such a terrible fright for her.

I remember the summers, they used to be so nice back then, much better than today, one could go for long walks without the worry of taking a coat in case it might rain, you can't seem to do that these days. I used to go blackberrying with my friends, we had a lot of fun, and it didn't matter that we would come home with our hands and arms full of scratches in our attempts to get big berries at the back of the bush.

We would go swimming together, I could not swim myself as I never learnt how to, so I would just get pushed in instead. My mum would never let me go to Midsummer Baths, because it was river water. Anyway, my Uncle Tom (mum's side) was the Lifeguard there, and I was so proud of him. Mum always knew if I had sneaked down there, I couldn't help it because it was open air and so nice down there. She would smell my costume to see if it smelt of river water or chloride from the nice New Baths on The Mounts.

Jean Osborn was my very best friend when I was growing up. Eileen was another good friend, who I still see today, as were Flossie Smith, Margaret Malin, Mary Norton, Pearl White and Mavis Haynes, all such good friends. Mavis's uncle used to have a horse and cart milk round and he would come along Green Street, my mum would take the jug out to be filled from the churn. No bottles of milk in those days.

There was also a Mr. Bird who used to have an oven at the back of his shop. He used to bake Yorkshire puddings for people on Sundays. I would go to get ours and it always amazed me how he knew whose pudding was who's. He got them out and moved them around with a long handled spade, the puddings were done to perfection.

The games we played as children were whip and top, my favourite, the faster we could get the top to spin made it exciting for us, we found a short leash was the best to get it spinning faster. We would also place three sticks against the wall with another stick across the top, the object of the game was to throw a ball at them, once down you took a pot shot at the others playing. Then there was Cannon, Rounders, Hide and Seek, which was a fun chase round the block. Statues where one of you was on with the others behind you. The one on would suddenly turn round and anyone moving was out.

When I was eight or nine, I had a baby doll's pram. Flossie Smith would come over and we would play houses. She would play with my doll's pram and I would ride her bicycle. I always wanted one, but mum wouldn't let me, I think it was because she feared for my safety. But then I had my dolls, Bonnie a big baby doll, a pair of twins, Shirley who had lovely gold hair. I still have Bonnie who sits in a chair upstairs with Susie my little black doll that my Aunties Ede and Elsie bought me. I was devoted to this one and told her all my secrets when I was growing up, she knew all my times of sadness and if I did badly at school.

My friends and I used to go down to the Fair when it came to Midsummer Meadow, it was great fun, I loved the Candy Floss and Toffee Apples. I also enjoyed the rides, they were so cheap then, only three pence a go. I used to play out every day, and would occasionally run inside for a slice of bread and jam and back out again. I didn't have a minute to live. We never had television then, we were always out playing with friends, Great Fun!

In 1947 the snow came, over four feet deep, this lasted for about nine weeks, a harsh winter. I left for school in wellingtons, I didn't want to go, mum stood watching me as I strode along Green Street, moaning about how the snow was going over the top of my wellingtons and down my legs, and how I can't get to school. She just answered that it wouldn't get any worse, it didn't, but I had a very cold day in school, yuk!

If we stayed away from school we would have the school board man come around on his bicycle to see why you weren't at school. The times he came around if I was at home, I'd hear his bike suddenly get propped up against the wall between Mrs. Clark's next door and our house, he'd go there first. I'd jump on the settee and mum would cover me up. When he came in she would say 'Look! She isn't at all well.' When he'd gone I'd jump off.

One thought comes to mind, Billy and I used to attend St. Peter's Church Sunday School, one day whilst inside we had stamps given for attendance, while Billy was putting his stamp in his book, John Steele, his friend, smiled and showed his book.

The caption read "Praise the Lord" and he'd written underneath "and pass the ammunition", a song of World War II. Well I couldn't help but giggle, I wasn't very old at that time. Up came Miss. Barker, an awesome sight! She was a

Victorian lady dressed in a long black coat which was high necked up to her throat with a large black hat. She got hold of me and said 'You blasphemous child,' shaking me she put me outside to go home. Well it was not really my fault, but I did have a giggle, as I was like that then you see. I never did like it and I didn't go back after that day for a long time.

Well then I moved on to the Blue School in Kingswell Street, I was eleven years old. On Sundays we had to attend Sunday School either at St. Katherine's Church or All Saints Church in the town centre. The only thing I can say about this school is that I hated it! Miss. Nobles was the headmistress and Miss. Brentnall was the cookery and housewifery teacher. Miss. Brentnall took it into her head that she didn't like Betty Waterfield, mind you I didn't like her either. We had to do fines, this meant we had to go into school at 6.00 a.m. and got buckets of coal and firelighters into all the rooms, we never had a caretaker back then, so we had to clean out all the ashes from the previous day's fire. I went in one horrible cold and wet morning with my friend Jean, she did the downstairs fires and I did the upstairs and the kitchen. Well, I cleaned out all the ashes, blackleaded the grates and polished all the brasses. Then I laid a good fire of wood and coal, before long it was all going merrily, everything was spick and span and I felt so proud of it all. The other girls came in at 8.30 and stood around the fire warming their hands and saying 'Oh what a lovely fire,' then in came Miss. Brentnall, she looked at the fire then at me because I was looking pleased with myself. She immediately got hold of the shovel and started to shovel out the fire, this caused black smoke and ash to fly everywhere, whist doing this she was screaming at me 'eight black marks for wasting coal'. She knew we had a points system for punishment and eight black marks meant you got the cane, and I was sent down for it. Miss. Nobles got the cane out and asked me why I was sent down so early in the day. I had to tell her I was given eight black marks for wasting coal. I stood there with my hands outstretched and the swish across them is too painful to describe! The cane hurt in more ways than one as the other girls cried out 'what a shame, Betty had made such a lovely fire,' but this all fell on deaf ears.

I earned a prize at that school for housewifery, the only thing was that Miss. Brentnall had to read it out and present it to me. She read out 'It is with real displeasure to say that Betty Waterfield has attained this'. A brooch lay on the table where earlier there had been lots of prizes. No one else had wanted the brooch, as they chose their prizes, so I went forth with my head held high, after all I had won it! I picked it up, turned around and went back to my seat.

We used to launder washing there too, we would do aprons and towels etc., there was no boiling then, we just laid them on long wooden table tops and scrubbed them with a brush and soap. Miss. Brentnall would walk past and hold them up to the light and scan them, more often than not she would throw them to the floor screaming 'do them again'. I thought she was a bit, well, loopy!

This is an excerpt from Betty's life story, which she completed in 2003, just before her death. She was a giggler to the end with a great sense of humour.

Tony Mallard 2007.

ST.MICHAEL'S ROAD

St.Michael's Road runs between Overstone Road and the Kettering Road. The north side of this street is dominated by a now defunct boot and shoe factory. These premises were built in 1876 and occupied firstly by Hornby & West and extended in 1883 and 1893 before being used by G.T.Hawkins from around 1912. The Company closed its doors for the last time in 1995 after around 120 years of successful trading. In its time it supplied riding boots to the Royal family, receiving a warrant in 1976. Boots for soldiers who fought in the Boer war, Korean War and the Falklands war were made as well as high-grade footwear for ladies and gents.

The history was unknown to me when I was a child and passed by four times a day on the way to and from school, St.Mary's Catholic School on The Mounts.

My most vivid memories of this factory are during hot summer days when all the windows would be open, the many machines would be thundering away, some just hammering, but others screeching, and there was such a strong smell of leather in the air. The main entrance to the building was in Overstone Road but there were two more in St.Michael's Road, again the good weather would bring out some of the workers during the lunch break to sit on the steps and enjoy their sandwiches or cigarettes. I was never around to see the start of the working day, but at the end of it the two streets thronged with people rushing to go home.

In those days, I am writing of the 1940's & 50's, the street had two-way traffic but it wasn't too busy with cars to stop the children being allowed out to play football or practise old time dancing in the road.

Also, what appeared to be almost a Sunday ritual was that housewives could be seen sweeping the pavement at the front

of their house and the doorsteps were almost white with the scrubbing.

Here is a picture of a Jumble sale dated probably around 1947, on the extreme left can be seen the edge of an air-raid shelter. Luckily I wrote on the back of the picture so I can tell who appears. *On the pavement, left to right; Mrs Lyle, Miss Bailey and Mrs.Withers.*

Children on the left Josephine Withers and Kitty Hodges.

Back row; Pam Haines, Irene Lyle, Shirley Haines and Jean Jeffs.

On the front row; Jean Lyle, David Jeffs and Peter the dog.

The street had three small food shops. At 21 was Crofts, this was next door to Hawkins and must have benefited from their workers trade. The next was ours at 37, Withers, although I believe it finished trading about 1948. The third was at number 55 and run by the Dobbs family. This one outlasted all and was still in operation in the 1960's and possibly even later.

I remember that a lady who lived at the Mounts end of the street used to 'take in' theatricals appearing at the New Theatre and promised me an introduction to Dorothy Squires. This never happened since Mum didn't wake me in time, and oh boy was I mad!

Another boot and shoemaker was Trickers, which at the time of writing (2006) is still in operation. This building is distinctive due to its' brown outer wall tiles and was recently used as a setting for the film Kinky Boots.

What is now the Spiritualist Church was the Church of the Latter Days Saints.

Jo Clements 2006.

SEMILONG - OR WAS IT THE BOROUGHS?

It wasn't until I was asked a very thought provoking question about my childhood that I started to think back and remember all the happy times, the days were long and filled with such fun and laughter.

I lived in Hampton Street for 19 years right up to the time I got married. I never could make out if we belonged to the Boroughs or Semilong.

In those days all the doors were left unlocked, often left open in fine weather, we would play tag, hopscotch, peep behind the curtains and of course marbles often playing this game in the gutters. In the autumn we had great fun playing conkers.

There was always someone you could run to if you fell off your bike or fell over, many of the ladies in the street were called auntie.

I will never forget Doll and Charlie Clarke who had the sweet shop and outdoor beer house at the top of the street. The shop was always packed with kids at school time buying a penny worth of kalihi, liquorice wood, cherry lips, sherbet dabs and lots more. We used to come out clutching our white paper cone shaped bags and do swapsies on the way to school.

School for many of us was St Georges, the headmistress was Miss Staughton, she was a real stickler for obedience.

There was Mr. North, Mr. Putsey, Mr. Markie and Miss Draper, I can't remember the other teachers, but I do know in later years after I married I found I was calling them by their first names, Arthur, Jim, Len, and Hilda, this was because my lovely mum (Betty Roberts) was now working at the school as secretary, will tell more about my mum in another story.

All of us kids from Hampton, Uppingham, Brook and Priory Streets were always down Paddy's Meadow playing on the swings, slides, roundabout and jazzer, many a time I can remember falling off the jazzer, we would make it go so high it would lock. We would take bottles of pop made from yellow kalihi from Charlie and Doll's shop and play for hours fishing, swimming and riding our bikes, unlike kids of today we always found fun things to do.

It was great on Bonfire night (Nov. 5th) for about 10 days prior to the event we would go round all the houses collecting rubbish for the 'Bonnie' that was always built in the meadow by the river. I remember that Brown's Garage along St Andrew's Road always donated the Guy and this would be displayed prior to the night outside their premises for 2 or 3 days. (Browns went on to be Brown's Haulage Company).

There was always rivalry between us and Spring Lane to see who could build the biggest 'Bonnie', and many a time each one was sabotaged before November 5th so we had to start again. On Nov. 5th all the families from the area would go down the meadow with their boxes of fireworks and sparklers and a great time was had by all, (those were the days).

As we grew older we ventured further afield, some of us went to the Racecourse and others to Victoria Park, even in those days we had our gangs but it was all friendly. If we wanted to be really adventurous we would trundle down to Castle Station packed with our pop and sandwiches and catch the train to Blisworth, it was so exciting going through Blizzy

16

Tunnel for the first time, with smoke from the funnel coming in through the open windows. When we arrived we would walk for miles blackberrying and playing games.

When I was 12/13 years old I realised I needed more spending money, so I went to Harry Harding's paper shop in Adelaide Street (that <u>was</u> Semilong) and asked if he had any paper rounds going. Luckily for me he had. I used to deliver after school to Adelaide St., Alliston Gardens, Gladstone Terrace, Northcote Street, Hester Street and Leslie Road. I loved the summer but delivering in the winter was very cold, but it was worth it with all my Christmas tips. Harry Harding along with his brother, I think his name was George, were real characters, but could be very grumpy at times.

There will always be one shop I will never forget and this was old Mrs.Briody's sweet shop in Grafton Street, (that certainly was in the Boroughs) the smell of her toffee used to entice kids in from all over, it was awesome, even now I can still smell the treacle, cloves and liquorice, tuppence worth of toffee, wow! Next door was old man Higginson's bike shop, this family always had trick bikes in the town's carnival, they were great. Lastly there was Sammy Warren's Fish and Chip shop, his chips and batter bits were something to die for.

Those days seemed longer and were packed full of fun and laughter.

Yes, those were the days.

Diane Banks
(formerly Roberts)   2007

CROSSING THE ROAD

Many years ago, when I was a young lad in the Cubs I was waiting to cross the Wellingborough Road near the Crown & Cushion pub to do a Bob-a-Job - cleaning the local butcher's bike who I believe was called Tysoe's.

Just along from me at the pavement's edge stood an old lady also waiting. In true Scout tradition I moved to join her and help her across. Before I could even take a step a passing car pulled up in the middle of the road. It was one of those 'sit up and beg' cars, probably an Austin Seven or similar. All the traffic, there wasn't much in those days, pulled up behind.

A man got out of the car, he was wearing a dark green suit and a trilby hat and had a small moustache if I recall correctly. He stepped over to the lady, lifted his hat, spoke a few words, took her arm and escorted her over the road. At the centre of the road he held up his free hand and the traffic coming the other way obligingly stopped. At the other kerb he once more raised his hat, spoke a few more words to the lady, re-crossed the road, got in his car and resumed his journey. All the other traffic moved off.

I only ever saw anything like this once, it must have been in the late 50s, I cannot imagine anyone doing it today. Apart from the fact that most car drivers have no manners whatsoever, especially where pedestrians are concerned, the man in the trilby would probably become a victim of road-rage!

Jack Plowman 2007

THE WAY THINGS WERE

In the times of the coal fire the coalmen used to deliver to your door weekly. The lorry would arrive and a man with very black clothes, black hands and face would put a full sack on his back and deliver it to the coal store, empty the sack and repeat the process depending on how much the family could afford. Almost everyone had a coal fire in those days, usually in just one room but, in times of sickness, the bedroom grate would be used too. These fires ensured work for the chimney sweeps. The furniture in the room would be covered and moved around to accommodate the extra space needed for the long flexible rods. The first one had a spiky black round brush that was pushed up the chimney then slowly more extension rods were screwed in until the brush appeared out of the top of the chimney pot. Pushing and pulling would produce a lot of soot in the living room and could take hours to clean up afterwards (we didn't have a vacuum cleaner). Of course another source of income for a sweep was to make an appearance at a wedding as it was thought to bring good luck to the happy couple.

If too many fires had burned before the sweep was called in a chimney fire could happen. This was heralded by burning soot dropping in the fire and then a great 'whoosh'. I remember my parents soaking sacks and holding them in the chimney to starve the oxygen, I was very young and frightened. While they were fighting the fire someone rang the doorbell, I was the only one free to answer only to be asked 'do you know your chimney is on fire?'

Coal fires produced a lot of ashes which had to be removed to stop the fire being choked, the ashes had to be cooled before going into the metal bin as you could easily set alight anything already in it. Ash-boxes, as they were known, were emptied by the dustmen twice a week.

Milk was delivered to your door daily, when I was very small the transport was horse drawn. The horse knew the round better than any new milkman and would guide him around. If you used the Co-op then you could buy milk checks from the store and leave them under empty bottles, which were always washed and left on the step, for payment. This also helped with the 'divi' payment made on production of your Co-op number (everyone remembers theirs, ours was 636) an early loyalty bonus scheme.

Another good service we used to have was that the postman would deliver twice daily and pillar boxes would be collected from at least twice daily too, and it was a one-class service, first class in more ways than one.

During times of illness a doctor would come out day or night, if you weren't that bad and could visit him then you could always be slotted in. The dispenser made up the medicine he prescribed in the surgery instantly.

Shop assistants would pass the time of day with you, would ask you what you would like, would get it, wrap it and even pack it for you, and still give you a smile.

Every night all the shops in the town centre would be a blaze of lights and people would walk up and down 'shop window gazing'.

Maybe they weren't all bad old days.

Jo Clements 2006.

SUNDAYS

My first recollection of Sundays was when I used to go with my dad very early in the morning to the farm where he worked. He was in charge of the massive incubators where they hatched the chickens and they were sent as day olds in cardboard boxes all over the country, but on Sundays dad had to take his turn, it was probably every other week, or one in three, can't remember, to go and feed and water the hens in the fields and collect the eggs. We used to go round in a van and I can remember getting out and holding the gates open when he drove through. I must have been aged between 5 and 10.

I also went to Sunday School at St. Mary's, Far Cotton on Sunday afternoons, but the only thing I can remember about that is our Sunday School Treat once a year when we all walked up Rothersthorpe Road to Danes Camp and we had races and played games and had tea in the field. I must have been very young then, because later on we used to go in a double decker bus to Wicksteed Park for our annual treat. I remember we used to go round the park on the train and also down the water chute and also went on the swings and slides, I know they had a massive long slide. We also went into the building for tea.

M.J.Cook. 2007.

ROYAL THEATRE

My best friend at school lived in Bedford Mansions in Derngate, where her mother was caretaker. Bedford Mansions is close to the Royal Theatre (or Rep as we used to call it) which made it popular with members of the company. One actor who lived there was Michael ffoulkes, who gave my friend's mum a couple of tickets for every production. Thus it was that two 14 year old schoolgirls were often to be seen in the best seats in the house, slap-bang in the middle of the front row of the Dress Circle.

We saw all sorts of things with our freebies, from the dated comedy Sailor Beware, to Shakespeare. Adam Faith was a big name in the Sixties, when he abandoned singing for acting. One of his first engagements brought him to Northampton to appear as Feste in 'As You Like It'. It was probably Michael ffoulkes who told Mrs Randall to take the two girls backstage to meet him after the performance. We were suddenly dumbstruck, and the meeting was a short episode of smiles and stilted conversation for both parties, but what could two teenagers from the backstreets of Northampton say to a household name? Mind you, we both noted that he was barely taller than the pair of us.

A couple of years later, Jo's family moved to another part of town, but we continued to go to the theatre regularly, and queue at the box office purses at the ready, and we continued to attend long after we left school. Eventually Jo and I lost touch, but I still go regularly, continuing a family tradition that began with my grandparents queuing in Swan Street for the Gods (gallery) from the 1920s.

Kate Wills

SCHOOLDAYS THROUGH ROSE COLOURED SPECTACLES

My first memories of school are probably seen through rose tinted spectacles but I look back on a happy time. As I was an only child growing up in a household with my parents, my paternal grand parents and my paternal great grandmother, to be with children of my own age and older was wonderful. As you can imagine at home I was pretty low in the pecking order. School days were fun. St Giles Church of England School was my first school and Miss Whitney was my first teacher. No mod cons there, outside toilets and no central heating, but we had a real fire with a fireguard and we would sit round the fire and drink our milk during the winter months. On Thursday morning we would walk in a 'crocodile' across St Giles Terrace to attend a church service in St Giles Church. It seemed very big and very dark. I think it still had gas lamps, but I enjoyed the service.

We celebrated May Day with a pageant.

I was old enough to join in and understand the celebration for the Queen's Coronation and I still have a red, white and blue striped propelling pencil with a crown on the end.

I was sad when the time came for me to leave St. Giles School but I soon settled in my new school Notre Dame High School and I only have good memories of my time there.

Val Knowles (nee Leach) 2008

NOTRE DAME HIGH SCHOOL

I have fond memories of the Notre Dame High School, as this was my school from 1942 to 1953. One of the best things I remember was the lovely garden, which we were allowed to walk round sometimes and also the beautiful chapel. We didn't go in there very often, as mainly the nuns used it, but we did go in on special occasions. We also had a very nice hall with a stage, and a beautiful wooden floor.

Sadly this building is no more, as it was pulled down in 1979 to make way for a row of very ordinary small shops. It was most commonly known as 'The Convent' and was towards the top of Abington Street on the left hand side looking towards Abington Square.

It was originally, since 1852, three houses in a pleasant residential district of Northampton with large gardens and fields in the vicinity, but these three houses in time became inadequate to house the number of children, which included boarders as well as day pupils and in 1870-71 work started on the new building and this was greatly extended over the years to come. Cows and sheep inhabited a large field and they also kept pigs, but in later years this land was turned into playing fields.

During the war a large number of children from coastal towns were evacuated to the Convent. The school became a Grammar School in 1945 and in 1950 the Boarding School was closed down, with only the Day School remaining.

This building was a prominent feature of Abington Street and it was a very sad day indeed for Northampton, the day they decided to pull this beautiful building down.

Mavis Cook 2006
Notes taken from Centenary Souvenir 1852-1952

BARRY ROAD SCHOOL DAYS

My three sons all attended Barry Road School during the '70's'. I remember making 'sock balls' to play football before school and at playtime. The boys were privileged to be pupils of a school with its own swimming pool, although the boys could all swim before they started school. My youngest son swam a width of the pool when he was just 18 months old. His brothers told him 'you get a watch if you swim a width'. He chose a 'Snoopey' watch.

Our house backed on to the school playground, so they didn't have far to walk to school, just round the corner. My middle son was the 'dreamer of the family', it would take him ages to get dressed and out of the door in time for the school bell. One evening when I checked the boys before I went to bed I noticed 'the dreamer' seemed to be very hot. On drawing back the duvet I found he had put his clean clothes on, including tie, under his pyjamas to save time in the morning.

Another day 'the dreamer' was particularly slow in getting ready for school, at last I managed to get him out of the door only for him to return after about 10 minutes. In exasperation I asked him why he was back.

He looked at me and said *"I haven't got my shoes on".* When I enquired why it had taken so long to get back home as it is all of two minutes to school, his answer left me speechless *"I didn't know until someone told me".*

During my eldest son's time at Barry Road the school system changed to three tier, Lower, Middle and Upper. Now during my grandchildren's education it has changed back to two tier again.

By Val Knowles 2008

MY GRANNY AND PAP

I remember as a young child going with my parents every Saturday evening to see my granny and pap, who seemed very old to me, but I don't suppose they thought of themselves as old as they would have been younger than I am now. We lived in Far Cotton and they lived in Spencer, so we had to catch two buses to get there and the same again home. I remember they had a very large table, which was an air raid shelter and it took up most of the space in the living room. They only had one room and a small scullery downstairs and two bedrooms upstairs. I don't remember seeing a bathroom, so I don't expect they had one, although they did have an indoor toilet, which had squares of newspaper cut up and hanging on a string for toilet paper. I used to play under the table, which I think was made of iron and had iron mesh on all sides to the floor.

My job when visiting them was to make spills out of old newspapers. These were used to light the gas cooker in the scullery, having been lit on the fire in the living room. Another job I used to have was to help my granny unravel old knitted garments, which we wound up into balls and she would knit something new with the wool. I also remember she had a coat which was very faded, so she unpicked all the stitching and turned the material round the other way and remade the coat. It was all 'make do and mend' in those days.

My pap had rheumatoid arthritis, so I only remember him walking with a stick. He used to go for a daily walk down to Victoria Park and back. I don't ever remember them going anywhere to visit anyone or for holidays and they only came to visit us one day a year and that was on Christmas Day, but I don't know how they got to Far Cotton. My pap used to give me a half crown for Christmas, but granny always had something for me hidden away.

They did have quite a large garden, where they grew vegetables and I remember they grew beautiful big chrysanthemums. I remember my pap had a stack of balls on the side, which had been kicked over his garden by the local children and he never gave them back.

When we went home from these visits, I used to have a treat of either hot chestnuts, or a baked potato, as these used to be cooked and sold on the Market Square in the evenings. I can remember the heat coming from the cart where they cooked them.

Mavis Cook 2007

THE BOX

My story begins when I was eleven years old and just starting my love of fishing. I had a fishing rod and reel, plus some floats, but no fishing basket to carry them in. As WW2 was still in progress, things were unobtainable or in very short supply and the chances of finding one were unlikely.

Then I found THE BOX. It was approximately 16"x12"x10" and having refitted the lid, I then planned to cut 3" off the longest measurement and fit two hinges to make a lid. Then disaster.....We had no saw (DIY had not been invented) Then as all mothers seem to do, mine had the answer, saying that if I took the box to Mr. Hallet and asked nicely and not bother him, he might cut it for me. Mr. & Mrs. Hallet lived a short distance away and were great friends of my parents and as I grew up, became friends of Pamela, my wife, and myself. In an instance I was at Mr. & Mrs. Hallet's explaining what was needed and how I was to make my fishing box. Mr. Hallet listened and must have noted all the pitfalls to my grand design, but said to leave the box and he would return it when he had time to cut it. As I slowly walked back home wondering, with impatience of youth, why could he not cut it while I waited, it would only take me two or three minutes and then I could finish the job for the next time I went fishing. One hour passed, then two, with my mood not improving and still no sign of Mr. Hallet. Then after three hours had elapsed, a knock at the front door. It was Mr. Hallet with THE BOX.

The top had been cut to make a lid as I had asked. He had also fitted a wide strip of webbing to make a rustless hinge, fitted a lip inside so the top had a snug fit, with a carrying strap of webbing and four small blocks for feet. All little things that I had overlooked or not even considered in my grand plan. But this is not the end of the story, he had upholstered the lid and covered it with some American cloth (to make it waterproof) and finished with round upholstered studs. The work or a true craftsman. To me it was a work of art. I felt like Izaac Walton, author of 'The Complete Angler' and would be the envy of all my friends.

I still have my fishing box with all my collection of fishing gear and at times still use it and as I sit at the side of the riverbank, I remember the kindness, friendship and the craftsmanship of both Mr. & Mrs. Hallet and how we can learn the skills and patience from our elders.

And to both a big THANK YOU...

Michael John Bull. 2000.

OUR MILKMAN

When I was a young lad before my Gran died (the only grandparent I ever really knew) we lived in Monks' Hall Road. This is a *cul-de-sac*, it runs off from Monks' Park Road and forms a right-angle, however there are alleyways (jitties) behind all the houses giving us kids plenty of places to run and play. It is possible to drive a car into the road and out along one of these jitties and come out further down Monks' Park Road.

Of course, before my school days I spent most of my time in the house or garden with, or within sight of, my mother. The highlight of the morning was when the milkman called. He didn't come very early so I think we must have been near the end of his round. I used to get the time pretty well right and then I'd hear him talking to his horse and then the milk cart would appear around the corner into our bit of the *cul-de-sac*.

Ken spoke more to his horse than to people, I recall. I remember he used to talk to my mum and I've wondered since if there was anything going on between them. However he seemed to like me, and mum sometimes gave him a cup of tea, so maybe he talked to her because of the tea or me – if anything was going on I'm sure it could only be flirting and at my age I wouldn't have known what that was.

The most interesting thing about him was his missing hand. I think he'd lost it during World War II and he had a *HOOK*! Being the age I was I wondered whether he was a superannuated pirate, only to find out from my mum about the war injury. I was warned not to draw attention to it as it might hurt his feelings, so I never did.

He used to have a galvanised iron wire bottle carrier that could hold, I think, up to eight bottles. He would load this up for the next two houses or so, hang it onto his hook and head off, whistling, up the paths to the front doorsteps, depositing the correct number of full bottles and collecting the empties. As he went from house to house the horse would amble along keeping pace with him and patiently wait always stopping at the exact same spot every day.

Why I was so keen to wait for Ken was that I was allowed to 'drive' the horse and cart. I think even at that age when I sat on that box-seat, holding the reins and feeling very important I knew I wasn't really in control and the horse did *just* what it always did!

Jack Plowman   2008

THE LAVATORY

Water Closets, Powder Rooms, Toilets, Rest Rooms, Convenience, are some of the names given to the lavatory.

My grandparent's lavatory (known as the privy) was situated at the bottom of their garden. It consisted of a bench made of wood with two smooth round holes placed side by side, presumably so that friends and family could pass the time of day whilst in use. Inside these holes were open-ended porcelain basins that allowed the waste to collect in a bucket which was then removed weekly by a local farmer, this sewage was then spread onto his fields. One of these fields was regularly used by my brother's scout troupe for their summer camp.

Only the most affluent homes had an inside toilet. In the majority of working class homes it was usual to have the lavatory placed outside the home adjacent to the back of the house. Often there were no water cisterns to flush the system so a bucket of water was usually placed outside the door for use when needed. A torch was also handy. Because of this arrangement, people not wanting to brave the elements during the night used a chamber pot. These chamber pots were used in most homes, they were placed under the bed, and could be known as the guzunder, the poe, the jerry and most vulgarly as the piss pot. It was a well-known remedy for chillblains to immerse the foot into the chamber pot and soak it in the urine. In some areas there was only one toilet which several families had to share.

There has been a variety of toilet paper. Discarded newspapers were once used, these newspapers were cut up into squares, and a hole punched into the corner and threaded through with string, and then hung on a nail within the lavatory. There was Izal toilet tissue that was more like greaseproof paper and then finally came the soft tissue that is in use today.

Pauline Etheridge

CHRISTMAS AT STANHOPE ROAD NORTHAMPTON 1970s

I have the most wonderful memories of Christmas with my Nan and Pap Allom in Stanhope Road. My grandmother was the most girlish grandmother anyone could have, from September onwards she would start to think of Christmas such was her love of it. She would start to write lists for the presents and each Saturday when she went to town from that point onwards, she would buy a present for some member of the family and cross it off her list.   Christmas puddings would be made in October, everyone had to have a stir and make a wish, then they would be greased, sealed and stored until they went into the steamer on Christmas Day, she always put a silver sixpence into each one.   Her Christmas cake was another joyful task, the icing always having a snow affect, she wasn't so good with a smooth finish. Her decorations and tree were a sight to behold.

We would go to my grandparent's house after opening our presents at home, there we would go down Queens Park Club on the corner of the street, a really smoky place, full of people of good cheer and sloppy kisses before leaving early with my grandmother to put the final touches to the Christmas lunch. We would squeeze around her dining table sitting on the most amazing assortment of chairs, anything that had legs and could bare our weight we sat on it.   There with our crackers, paper hats, grandad's home made wine, we would tuck into our very special meal. I always made sure that I never sat next to my great grandmother as she had a habit of passing food that she didn't like onto the unfortunate person's plate sitting next to her, saying 'you eat this my duck, shame to see it go to waste.' This was a great irritation to my grandmother who would then send looks to my grandfather saying, 'please do something about your mother.' Those that sat next to the coal fire scorched, those that sat next to the hall door froze.

Following the endless washing-up, no dishwashers in those days, the adults would then retire to watch the Queen's speech. Us children became very bored once they dozed off, they often lost the Christmas spirit as we fell or tripped onto their prostrate forms. My grandmother always had a basket full of chocolate, it was wonderful deciding which bar to choose.

Then the rest of the family would come for tea, out would come another enormous spread of food that no one really wanted because they were still full from lunchtime. We would play Ludo, dance to the latest chart music, do the 'bump' which everyone thought was hilarious, the children would cry as another pair of adult feet destroyed a new toy left on the floor, until the time came for all the men to play cards whilst the women got the supper – more food. At the end of another wonderful Christmas day, everyone would wrap up from head to foot, before waddling home, slightly merry, pushing prams, carrying toddlers, no one had cars then, looking forward to tomorrow, Boxing day, when exactly the same would happen, the only difference being the venue, my uncle's house instead of my grandparents.

My grandmother has left her legacy to most of her children and grandchildren, her love of Christmas, my mother has a big family Christmas party each year, when I ask my teenage son what he wants for Christmas, his usual reply is a big family party.

Penny Etheridge 2007

ABINGTON STREET- CHRISTMAS TIME

When I was a lad, I'm not sure of my age, but I was at secondary school ("Kett's Kollege for Kool Kats" circa 1957 - 1961) I can remember going into town with my mum shortly before Christmas.

It was a great secret, but like most kids I had a good idea of what I was going to get for Christmas. I always got the Eagle Annual, which I had (and still have) from numbers 1 to 9. By then I was beginning to get too old even for the 'boys' newspaper' - it was *never* considered a comic such as the Beano or Dandy; these were looked down upon with distain by my contemporaries and myself - however, we still read them! Hulton Press, the publishers of the Eagle, Girl, Robin and Swift were taken over by Odhams Press who ruined all four publications by inserting advertisements and 'dumbing them down' - so this seemed a good time to stop subscribing to it.

What I had always wanted, but never, got was the largest of the Meccanno sets, I think it was No. 1. This came in a wooden chest instead of a cardboard box with several drawers and included some of everything Meccano offered, including a *clock-work motor* - boy, what could I have built with that! It cost a huge amount, I think something like 10 guineas so it was always out of reach.

During the year I would look at such a prize in the catalogue and dream as to how I could raise the money, for I knew my parents would never be able to afford to buy it for me, but at Christmas you could visit Johnson's Store in Abington Street and see the real thing on display. Although Johnson's sold other things such as sports equipment, it was, to me, *the* premier toy store. Along with the usual dolls and footballs it sold the *real* stuff - Meccano, microscopes, chemistry sets and optical and electrical gadgets.

The large window was devoted each Christmas to a model mountain scene with a railway running up and around it. In the window frame was set a metal plate with a slot in it, covered all year but for this season. The insertion of a penny into this slot would cause the train to run around the track for a few circuits and the money, I think, went to the local hospital.

Another regular feature of the Christmas season was over the road in the railed off space before the Notre Dame. Every year the nuns assembled a stable with all the usual figures associated with the Nativity; baby Jesus, Mary and Joseph, Wise Men, shepherds and assorted sheep, oxen and other beasts.

Each year brought something different to Abington Street and then one year it brought Christmas lights, once used, I seem to recall, in Regents Street, but to me the things that remained constant indicators of the season were the nuns' Crib, Johnson's electric train display and a view of that much wished for No. 1 Meccano set!

Jack Plowman   2007.

Chapter 2
MORE ON ABINGTON STREET
AND LATER MEMORIES

ABINGTON STREET (1)

Abington Street featured in every aspect of my childhood and teens. I was born in Lady's Lane, which ran parallel to the north of Abington Street. I had to cross Abington Street to reach my first school, St. Giles, and my second school, Notre Dame High School, was in Abington Street, and in my late teens I would walk along Abington Street from the Royal Theatre in Guildhall Road to get home.

I felt very safe whatever time of day or night, as there were always lots of people about, with the pubs, restaurants and New Theatre open in the evenings and all the lovely shops during the day. It was a major artery carrying the town's life blood in and out of town. Just a few months ago I had occasion to walk along Abington Street at 7 p.m. and it was desolate and quite frightening, a ghost town. The heart has been torn out of our town.

Val Knowles 2007.

ABINGTON STREET (2)

Number 63 Abington Street in the 1950's 60's and 70's was Dolland & Aitchison Ltd., Photographic Cameras and Materials.

On Saturday mornings it was a very popular destination for photographers like myself to purchase our photographic needs and meet other keen photographers like myself.

After a time it became a regular stop over and a few of us were allowed to congregate in the small room downstairs that stored some of the larger equipment, thanks to Reg the manager and sometimes we had the luxury of a tea or coffee, thanks to Reg's assistant.

It became like a mini club and we would exchange views on cameras and equipment etc. (as well as setting the world to rights) plus discussing our needs with Reg or Betty his assistant and handle a camera or enlarger etc. before making our choice.   Oh for those days of shopping. Not like today where all you have is a sealed pack and not knowing what the product is like and if you ask an assistant the usual answer is, 'I don't know, I only work here.'

Michael John Bull

ABINGTON STREET (3)

My earliest memories of Abington Street are only from 1983, when buses still ran down the street, and one could get off near the Market Square, instead of negotiating the Grosvenor Centre.

Most of the desecration had already been done by then.   Today there are only two listed buildings, the corner of the Market Square (now Phones 4U) and the library. Walking up the street now and looking above the shops, very little of interest remains, but I have noticed above nearby shops what looks like original brickwork, stone, and stone heads, the design has been emulated and incorporated into the Peacock Place entrance. That is another conundrum, I first knew Peacock Place as an alley-way of shops connecting Abington Street and the Market Square, so how is it now on a slope, with escalators and glass lifts connecting the two levels, with all their empty shops

Another old building remaining on the corner of Fish Street is what was Clays the butchers and is now 'chocolate heaven.' As one of the few old buildings left, why isn't that listed? Then there is the old doorway on the corner of Albert Place

(spoiled by a steel security door) that should be preserved.

I am glad the trees in the street are maturing, they hide the monstrosities put in place of the interesting and sometimes beautiful buildings that have now gone. Looking at old photographs and maps, I am sad that I didn't know Northampton pre 1970's.

A Saunders 2007

GAYEWAY 1958
ROCK AND ROLL DANCE HALL

Gayeway itself was a very basic place, a cross between a disco and youth club. The average age when I went there was 16 years. To us who were so attracted to it, it was magical, a place to meet friends, dance and have fun. We were able to dance and listen to the latest chart music which was very often frowned upon at home. We experimented with fashion, make up and hairstyles, so different from the classroom. A place where we were able to spread our wings and meet kids from other areas of the town, to meet the opposite sex, mostly, in this period schools were single sex so the opportunities to mix with the opposite sex were very few .We fell in love for the first time, experienced broken hearts, became aware of ourselves and for many forming life long friendships.

Gayeway was the brainwave of Ron Stanley, a man born before his time regarding the dance and entertainment field, he and his wife Jean Smith both professional ballroom dancers, saw the need and potential for places where young people could dance, particularly modern dance, and especially Rock and Roll. They held weekly dances in most of the Co-operative halls around the town catering, for the late teens and early twenties age group. The most popular was held on a Saturday night at the Exeter Hall. They then acquired premises in Abington Street, setting up Gayeway which attracted a younger age group. Ron and Jean were very friendly and took great interest in us kids, forming good relations with us all, it was such a happy place. Ron would stand no nonsense, he was very strict, if you ever caused trouble then you knew that you would never be allowed to go to visit Gayeway again. This was a thoroughly decent place, fights or drugs never happened there. We had great respect for them both. I remember on my 16th birthday, Ron phoning me up and playing 'Happy birthday sweet sixteen' something that I will always remember.

To gain entry into Gayeway you walked through tall gates directly off Abington Street into a small courtyard leading into the dance hall. As mentioned before the premises were very raw. Immediately inside was a long counter which sold soft drinks including the new drink of the day 'coca cola', bottled, not canned, snacks, sweets and 'Rothman' king size cigarettes which sold for 2d each. The seating were benches which were old and upholstered and came from discarded coaches, these were placed along one wall similar to a cinema layout. The walls were plain bricks or breezeblocks painted white, the floor was wooden. Lighting varied with whichever dance was happening, bright for Rock and Roll dimming when the slow music came on.

The blare of Rock and Roll music always greeted you, It may have been Little Richard, Chuck Berry, Buddy Holly to name just a few from the many incredible pop stars which were making names for themselves at this time. Bill Haley's era had passed. Elvis was our hero and mentor, boys would dress like him, wearing crepe soled shoe, drainpipe trousers, draped jackets, sporting DA haircuts, (the hair was swept up both sides forming a quiff similar to a duck's backside).

This was also the era of teenage fashion. We would arrive with tissues stuffed down our bras, no padded bras then, full skirts which underneath we wore starched, boned net petticoats. Sugar water was also used to harden these petticoats, this was also handy for keeping fancy hairstyles in place. Most Saturdays I would make a dress to wear that night from material which I had bought from 'Fatty' on the market (no political correctness then) for 2/6d a yard. Cardigans were worn back to front, poppet beads were all the rage. Strong elasticated belts were worn around our tiny 19 inch waists. Roll-ons – a strong elasticated type of corset, which you had to step into and then roll up your legs, held in the stomach, this certainly reduced the hip area, but often stopped the lower body functioning normally. The alternative to these was suspender belts and stockings or white socks known as 'bobby socks', no one ever went bare legged. The first shops appeared that catered for teenagers. Baby doll pyjamas, American tan tights became available, flat heeled or stiletto shoes adorned our feet.

Our makeup consisted of Panstick foundation, baby pink lipstick, brightly coloured eye shadow, black eyeliner and block mascara. To apply this mascara you needed to wet or spit onto this black substance to moisturise it turning it into a thick paste, this was then applied to the eyelashes via a small flat brush. Hairstyles were beehives, flick ups or ponytails., The boys were as vain as us girls with their clothes and hairstyles. I know a man who now confesses to wearing two pairs of trousers at the same time because his legs were so thin.

We would jive non- stop to all our favourite music, swirling skirts, ponytails and poppet-beads swinging as we were spun around, never tiring. The boys were incredible dancers, bopping and catching us as we danced with them. Life was fun, exciting. The lights would dim when the slow ballads came on, instantly most would pair off and we would creep around the floor smooching to the soft romantic songs, the Everley Bros, the Platters, even Cliff Richard sometimes, we mostly preferred the American artists, their music was far more exciting.

I feel so happy that I went to Gayeway, and also very lucky that I was young and carefree at this exciting and liberated time of the early 60's.

Polly Allom 2007

My Memories of Ron Stanley and Gayeway

In the early years of the 1950s when young people decided to go dancing they had to learn ballroom dancing because there was no real alternative in this town.

*Ron
Stanley*

At the time Ron Stanley ran a club that gave instruction in ballroom dancing at the old Gaumont Cinema on the Market Square. I was too young to take advantage of this, but in the mid 50s Ron set up in some of the Co-operative Halls giving ballroom instruction on the quick step, waltz etc. I started to go to the Co-op hall in St.Leonards Road, Far Cotton with my friends, this instruction was rather short lived because at the time the first Rock and Roll records were coming onto the market and young people had already a taste of this because 'Rock around the Clock' was the main theme of the popular film 'Blackboard Jungle' in 1954. Ron saw the potential of this music and expanded to run the dances at various Co-operative halls in the town. To take advantage of this vibrant and exciting new music, his dances consisted of 20 minutes of Rock and Roll followed by 10 minutes of the Creep dance with the lights out, so you could get to know the girls, the evening ran from 8 – 10 pm weekdays and until 10.30 pm on Saturdays.

*Teddy   Boys
(young boys
   of that era)*

In the fifties there was, like today, trouble caused by a minority of the youth but Ron would have no truck with any troublemakers and laid down firm laws and it was not past him to eject troublemakers himself. At the time Gayeway was the only venue that you could dance to Rock and Roll and the young people soon realized that if you wanted to go there you had better behave or you would be barred. Saturday night at the Exeter Hall in Exeter Road was the highlight of the week. This hall was situated in the terraced, streets that at the time ran between the Wellingborough and Kettering Road to be replaced by flats and a new Exeter Hall that has now been demolished.

Ron was firm and fair and developed a thriving club. He started to arrange trips to see the American Rock and Roll stars who were starting to tour this country. I remember going to see 'Bill Haley and the Comets' at the height of their fame, it was a magical night.

Although Rock and Roll was very popular you rarely heard it on the radio or T.V apart from Radio Luxemburg, but at Gayeway you could always hear the latest records, where Ron got them from was amazing.

As other people started to realize the potential of this music other venues started to open up and cafés dedicated to the young people started to appear. Lynn's Café in the Lower Mounts was one of the most popular.

Northampton was very lucky to have Ron Stanley and Gayeways, a name at the time reflected the true meaning of the word.

John Andrews

JIVE BY CANDLELIGHT

More years ago than I care to remember I started working for a sign-makers in town. I was the youngest working there and the other three young chaps suggested on my second or third week after they'd got to know me that I went with them to the YMCA on Friday night to 'pick up some girls'. I'd never been to a dance before so it was with a certain level of trepidation I met the other three chaps uncomfortably dressed in my one and only suit. Although this was just at the end of the Teddy-boy era we dressed in more conventional suits without 'drape coats'.

The YMCA building in Cheyne Walk has now been demolished but at that time it was new and modern. At the rear of the building was a huge [to me] hall and in here music was playing and the lights were dim. This was because along each long wall were small round tables with chairs and on each table was a bottle with a lit candle, this apart from the light coming from the lobby was the only illumination. However, once we had been in there for a while our eyes got used to the light.

Along the right side as you went in the tables and chairs were occupied by lads like us and on the right stood or sat the girls. Once we had settled in and fortified ourselves with a Coke and met some more mates we began to look at the girls opposite. They, in turn were eyeing us up, pointing and giggling. My companions filled me in on the procedure, explaining that you sauntered over to a girl you liked and asked her to dance – and there you were! I protested that I knew nothing about dancing especially how to jive. They brushed this aside saying that they couldn't either – in fact most of the guys and the girls couldn't dance properly either, all you do is giggle about and 'chat her up.'

I now realise that although I received much encouragement to make my play, none of the chaps I was with actually were going over to the girls. Finally three or four of us plucked up courage [safety in numbers!] and made our way over the floor. The distance seemed immense and the walk seemed to take ages while I felt that everybody's eyes were on me. I can't remember anything about the girl I had 'selected' and I suffered the humiliation of being turned down and as I started on the long walk back the greater humiliation of the sound of several girls giggling.

When I got back to 'safety' with my mates they at least congratulated me on trying and my shame was lessened by observing that only one of us had scored and that only lasted for one dance. We finished off the night by going to a pub where I tried a pint of beer with my mates. This, at least, I knew about, having been introduced to beer when I was quite young. At the time I didn't appreciate its bitter taste and drank by choice cider, but on that night I stuck to what the lads were drinking. I never went back to the YMCA's 'Jive by Candlelight'.

Jack Plowman 2008

MOMENTS IN HISTORY

Moments in history that have happened in my time are many, but I have seen two coronations. The first was King George VI on 12th May 1937, at the time I was only five years old, but remember being dressed in a suit made from a union jack flag. Plus all the usual street parties with pop and cakes made by ladies of Essex Street, as no one had shop cakes in those days.

All the children were presented with a coronation cup as a souvenir (I wonder where mine is now???)

I remember Mr. Barker of Essex Street making hot air balloons of wire and tissue paper and sending them up into the air from the church grounds, the first one accidentally went up in flames, but the others sailed away into the air over the church.

The second on June 3rd 1953 (The year I was married. Does this count as a historical event?) Returning from our honeymoon we spent two days with Pam's aunt and uncle in London sight seeing … Hyde Park, The Mall etc. with all the regalia of the coronation.

ON THE BALCONY OF BUCKINGHAM PALACE

THE CORONATION OF HER MAJESTY QUEEN ELIZABETH.

A TUCK CARD

. Returning to Northampton in time for the street parties. Then back to work at Raphael Tucks photographic post card department on night shift for three weeks printing thousands of Coronation photographs for the shops. What a way to start married life? Still we seem to have survived.

Apart from two Coronations I lived through WWII with its air raids, rationing, yanks, evacuees, the home guard to name a few. It was a completely different way of life from today, with the coming of TV, mobile phones, holidays abroad, The Beatles, pop concerts and the motor car.

Michael John Bull 2008.

Chapter 3
PEOPLE REMEMBERED

MY GRANDPARENTS
William and Emily Jane Allom (Ward)

My grandfather was born in 1883, a military man. I cannot ever remember him being jolly, he always_appeared serious and mostly silent. He came to Northampton from the East End of London looking for  work and eventually joined the Northampton Regiment stationed at the Army Barracks in Barrack Road and so started his army career, eventually he became a Sergeant Major

As a young soldier he was stationed in Africa and he always said of his time there that he had never seen such a happy, contented race, that he said, was before the arrival of the white man.

He and my grandmother, who was born in Northampton, travelled and lived in Malta (where my father and uncle were born), Gibraltar, Egypt and India. My grandmother so used to servants, became the most hopeless housewife, so my grandfather took over the role as housekeeper once he retired from the army.

INDIA 1911

Northamptonshire Regiment

He continued to wear uniforms while working during his retirement. For a time he worked as a cinema commissionaire, there he wore full dress uniform which was decorated with braiding, brass buttons, and epaulettes, even a cap. He also worked for an undertaker, dressed in black, complete with a high top hat. Once during this time my grandmother asked how a certain bride looked, he replied 'I don't know, brides and corpses all look the same to me.' So perhaps he did have a sense of humour.

My grandfather was one of the early motor owners and would say that he could drive to Bugbrooke and back, where my other grandparents lived, and only see two other cars on the road. Once when he bought a new car, this was a time when all cars were black and looked the same, parked at Overstone Solarium and because he forgot exactly where he had parked and failed to remember his number plate had to wait for the car park to empty before he could leave for home.

In his eighties he would sit outside his house in Kerr Street in his Austin 6, listening to his transistor radio wearing a panama hat, kid gloves and linen jacket watching the world go by. Sadly this was his end because he fell whilst getting out of the car, broke his hip and developed pneumonia.

Brevitt's Shoe Factory celebrating
King George VI's Coronation

My grandmother, born in the Boroughs, was the complete opposite to my grandfather and was the life and soul of any gathering. When she returned to Northampton following my grandfather's retirement from the army, not being able to settle as a housewife, went to work at Brevitt's shoe factory. She worked next to a French lady there and became fluent in french, she was still able to speak this language when she was in her nineties. She loved her working life, this was not necessary financially, but the company was. Her house seemed very dark, as were most houses, she was a hoarder and loved antiques. I would sit and watch her comb thick black dye through her long hair that she wore in a bun. She was a tiny lady with size 3 feet. She loved cats and welcomed all the local strays into her garden where she fed and cared for them. Her small walled garden certainly didn't smell of roses.

I will never forget one Christmas Eve afternoon when I met her rushing down Wood Street, she said that she hadn't realised that it was Christmas Eve, so was heading towards the market to buy a chicken for the Christmas Day meal.

In later years, (she lived to be 103 years old) I would take her to her sister's house each week, where they, plus two elderly neighbours, would meet. On the doorstep would be a crate of Guinness and two bottles of sherry. During the afternoon they would get happily merry and sing around the piano.

She sadly outlived all her friends and said that she would have to be pole axed, she died by choking on a sandwich in St Edmund's Hospital. When she knew that she was to be admitted into St.Edmund's Hospital she became distraught due to associating it to the workhouse. I remember visiting her there; she was convinced that she was covered in fleabites.

I will always remember my grandmother for her generosity, her kindness towards her fellow beings and her love of life. She said that her longevity was due to drinking a Guinness a day, always out of the bottle, because she said that it tasted better that way.

Polly Allom   2007

MY FATHER

My father, Albert Edward Bull, lived his life in Semilong from a boy until he was married. He lived in Essex Street, apart from a short time when he lived with his grandparents in Colwyn Road.

As a lad he seemed to have done most of the things that young lads of the time did. I recall him telling me how they used to tie two adjoining door knobs together so the owners could not open the doors, then knock on the doors and run. Also they used to swing from a rope tied to a gas lamp-post and how Sgt. Powell, who lived at the lower end of Essex Street, used to chase them over the open ground at the bottom of the street. They would hide in holes they had dug as dens. Sgt. Powell would leap over the dens and make out he had lost them, all in fun. Another time they lit a bonfire and went over to the allotments, crawled along the rows of potatoes, scrabbled out the ground, took the odd potato and then covered the roots so as not to be found out. Back at the bonfire with the potatoes nicely cooked, a deep voice asked where they had got the potatoes from (it was Sgt. Powell again) 'from our mums' vegetable baskets' was the answer. 'Oh, not from the allotments then?' asked Sgt. Powell. HE KNEW. 'No, No!' came the reply. 'Right then, if they are cooked, I'll have one,' so doing he took the

largest and went off mumbling, 'next time, make sure
you get some salt from your mums' kitchens.'

As a young man, my father was known for his natty
attire, with his smart hat and black cane with silver top,
to the extent of being nicknamed 'Pimp'. Years later,
when he worked on the buses, his nickname was 'Tich',
after the music hall entertainer Little Tich – my dad was
only 5'1. As a young man he would go out with the local
lads, as young men do. One of his best friends was the
son of Hillier's the butchers, of 110 Kingsthorpe Hollow
and as he had to work for his dad in the shop until late
they would all meet at the shop and wait for him to finish
work, when they left to go on the town, old Mr. Hillier
would cut them all a piece of raw suet to eat on the way.

In the war, as an ARP Warden, he became known as 'Sarge' to all the firewatchers. When he retired he did the milk round for Bill Horn on the corner of Agnes Road and became known as 'The Flying Milkman'. Although only small, he could nip around at a fast pace.

Michael John Bull

ALFRED C. KNIGHT

Alfred Charles Knight was born May 5th 1918. His mother was my great aunt Eleanor (nee Harrison) born in Olney. When Uncle Alf was born he lived at the bottom of Woolmonger Street with his mother, father and two brothers. I do not know how long they lived there but I recall Uncle Alf telling me that the house was small with two bedrooms, and it was very damp. One night when the family was in bed there was a terrific crash, the whole house shook, it appeared the whole rear wall had collapsed.

They were re-housed in Britton Road where the rest of the family lived until, in Uncle Alf's case, his marriage to Patricia Harrison (no relation). His brothers and his mother and father continued living in Saxon Street until their deaths. Uncle Alf and his wife were then allocated a house in Beechcroft Gardens where they brought up five children, little Pat, Steven, Veronica, Barbara and Michael. Uncle Alf served in the army in WW2 and was a bodybuilder and weightlifter. He was asked to compete for England in the 1948 Olympics and won a bronze medal for weightlifting. He married Patricia in 1949. When he left the army and returned to Northampton he worked for the Co-op as slaughterman before going into the licensing trade. He was landlord of the Welcome Tavern on Crane Hill and then the Queen's Arms on the Market Square. There was a photo published in the Chronicle and Echo of Uncle Alf lifting Auntie Pat up in the crook of his arm when they married, she was no light slip of a girl either. As well as being a landlord, he also ran a gym and keep fit club in Fetter Street with his youngest son Michael. He was always looking for the next Olympic champion I believe. When he retired, his years of using his legs and muscles left him unable to walk, Aunt Pat was unable to look after him, as she was not in the best of health herself. They celebrated their Golden Wedding anniversary in 1999. Uncle Alf went to Obelisk House, where my mother was, and on the 18th July 2000 he passed away.

A funeral was held at the church of St Peter and St Paul in Abington Park and hundreds who knew him attended it. He was an unassuming man, always ready for a laugh and to help others but he would not be put on. He knew most of the top boxers of the day including Freddie Mills, when we visited him there was usually someone there, notable of the sporting world. Many people still know of Alf Knight, he will be missed for years to come.

Mike Papworth

CANON L.A. EWART

An interesting character connected with the New Theatre in Abington Street was Canon L.A. Ewart. Canon Ewart was appointed vicar of Earls Barton church in 1930 and he raised large sums of money for the preservation of the historic Saxon church, but he was also known as a magician and escaper and performed at the New Theatre. He learned the art of escaping when he was a prison chaplain in Birmingham. He was also chaplain to

Northampton New Theatre and Northampton Repertory Theatre.

M.J.Cook 2007

MY DAD A PROJECTIONIST

When I was in my early teens in the mid 1950's, my dad worked for the Cipin brothers, Sydney and Myer, as a projectionist, they owned the Ritz, Plaza and Tivoli Cinemas.

Dad worked at the Tivoli on the corner of Main Road in Far Cotton. The hours were long and sometimes he worked seven days a week.

The smaller cinemas ran old films and the modern films that had already been run at the two major cinemas, the Gaumont on the Market Parade, and the Savoy on Abington Square.

Sometimes the older films would break and then it would be whistling, stamping and cries of 'why are we waiting?'

They ran two films each session, plus newsreels, trailers and adverts. The programme was changed twice a week, Monday - Wednesday and Thursday - Saturday with a different show on Sundays.

I enjoyed my dad working at the cinema as he was given free entry tickets which he gave to me, so instead of going to the cinema once a week, I went two or three times. I mainly went to the Ritz in Kingsthorpe as this was my local cinema.

The funny thing is, although my dad worked as a projectionist, he didn't actually like watching films and I can only remember him going to the cinema once.

Linda Kemp 2008

THOMAS WILLIAM BURNELL, 1854 – 1919; CHIMNEY SWEEP

Thomas W Burnell 2nd from the left

Thomas William Burnell was my grandfather on my mother's side, born in 1854 in Northampton. He was one of four brothers and two sisters. The brothers and my great-grandfather lived in Broad Street with my great-grandmother, who looked after the business-side, while the menfolk did all the chimney-sweeping. He later married my grandmother, who came from Berkhamstead, and set-up his own business, plus bringing-up six girls and one son.

His chimney sweeping was quite successful, with local houses and the old prison chimneys to sweep, and travelling further afield in his pony and trap to some of the big houses and estates in the country. He stored soot in the stable loft to sell to the farmers, who spread it on the land to help kills some the bugs and the like.

He had to keep an accurate record of all his sweepings by law, in case anyone had a chimney fire. Chimney fires were potentially very serious, as fire could spread very quickly, putting many homes in danger. A chimney fire brought many otherwise honest residents before the magistrates, who would usually impose a small fine.

He died in 1919, soon after the First World War, long before I was born, but from stories my mother told me he must have been quite a character. I would loved to have met him.

He could often be seen sitting on his front doorstep, talking to the vicar of St Edmund's Church (in Wellingborough Road, now demolished) talking sport and setting the world to rights. I never heard my mother say he was a big churchgoer but the vicar and he were great friends. My grandmother and the girls were all in the Salvation Army at times, with grandmother playing in the Market Street Salvation Army Band, and my Aunt Ethel becoming a lieutenant-colonel, and serving in the Salvation Army in Bermuda and Canada – but that is another story.

Grandfather loved to go to the home games at The Cobblers, and at the final whistle-time one of the girls had to go to the top of St Edmund's Road to find out the score. If The Cobblers had won, they would run home to tell my mother to put the cooking pot on, as they knew they would be having smoked haddock for tea. If they lost, it would be anything from the larder.

He must have been very strict with their upbringing, as my mother related that if anytime someone misbehaved at the meal-table, off would come his bowler hat, and the rim came down on the bridge of your nose. Mother said you never played-up at the meal-table more than once.

Since starting to write about my grandfather, I have discovered he was a sergeant in the St. John Ambulance Brigade, and he went on many manoeuvres with the Army summer camps, with fellow St. John comrades, who seem to have cooked for the soldiers. I am trying to find out more about him, and if I'm lucky I will be able to add to this story.

Michael John Bull 2008

A ROYAL HUNTING REMINISCENCE.

My grandfather, George Withers, died in December 1937 and the following letter appeared in the Northampton Independent.

The death of Mr. George Withers, the noted Northampton dog fancier, has recalled to a correspondent an amusing incident in which the present King, when Duke of York, took part.

It happened on a morning when the Pytchley were holding their opening meet.

Mr.Withers was standing on the road-side leading to Brixworth, accompanied by his faithful, battle-scarred terrier-the hero of a thousand fights with badgers and other dogs-waiting for a friend who had promised to pick him up in a car. My correspondent came along in a car and offered to give Mr.Withers a lift, which he accepted, little imagining the important part he and his terrier were due to play in the fortunes of the Pytchley that day.

After a fox had been bolted from Holcot covert, Reynard sought refuge in a drain beneath the road. The hunt was held up, for the huntsman had not brought the little terrier usually carried for bolting purposes.

A girl came along with a fox terrier puppy, which was commandeered by the Hunt, but was found useless. Whereupon my correspondent urged Mr.Withers to go to the rescue with his old warrior. Eventually he jumped from the car with his dog and descended to the mouth of the drain in the deep hedgerow.

Seated on their hunters in the road above were the Duke of York, the Masters of the Hunt, and many distinguished followers. One of the Masters shouted to Mr.Withers: "Do you think your dog can manage to bolt the fox?"

Mr.Withers looked up with scornful surprise, and remarked, "Manage, indeed! You just wait a minute and you'll see."

Then, putting his dog in the drain with a few encouraging words, the onlookers waited in eager suspense, but not for long. Suddenly there was a hue and cry. The fox had bolted from the other end of the drain and gave the Hunt a rattling run, which was recorded in all the National papers on the following day.

As the reports paid tribute to the timely service rendered by "Mr.George Withers, of Northampton, the noted breeder of Sealyham champions," he received letters from all over the country asking for puppies of the dog that had helped give the Duke of York and the Pytchley such a splendid start to the season.

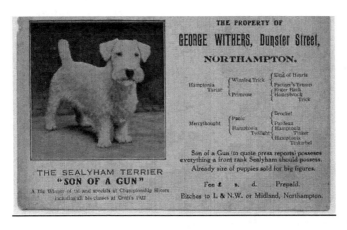

J.M.Clements 2006

MEAT 'N' POTATOES WITH 'RAILINGS' ROUND

c.1913

The 'railings' consisted of a crust of pastry pressed around the inside of a baking tin in which were laid some meat, with sliced onions, potatoes and gravy. Sometimes a hock and suet pudding were used and this was called 'ock n dough'.

Alice and Henry Westley with their five daughters c.1913

From L-R back row Alice, Ida, Gladys, Henry

From L-R front row Margaret, Elsie, Phyllis

As a schoolgirl, it was my Aunt Gladys's job to take the meat 'n' potatoes with the 'railings' round to the bakehouse before school, pick up the dish when cooked and deliver it to her Westley cousins, Amy and Harry, so that they would not be forced to go into the workhouse. They had become destitute following the death of their mother, and their father was unable to keep them. My grandmother, Alice Westley, when she heard of their plight exclaimed no relative of hers would go into the workhouse, and so sent them this daily meal. The teacher scolded my aunt for being late for school even though she had been doing her 'duty'. The Westley cousins later moved into my grandmother's house and Harry went off to the first world war. When he returned, he was shell-shocked and couldn't settle. Like many returned soldiers he took to the road and became homeless.

The Westley's grandparents originally came from Brayfield on the Green and worked in the shoe trade. They were married at Little Houghton and moved to Northampton. The family lived at 1 St. Giles Terrace, then moved to Jubilee Mews, Alma Street, School Terrace and Oliver Street, Kingsley Park before settling down in Greenwood Road, St. James where my grandmother lived with her husband Henry Westley and their five daughters. Henry was a shop steward at Padmore & Barnes, the shoe factory, but used to go to C & E Lewis's shoe factory where he would rattle a button box to encourage people to put money in it. He was known as 'mad' Henry but actually he was very clever. He was a member of the group who started the first political party that became the Labour party. Alice, known as 'Ginny' was pretty and partial to a drop of gin. She would sit at a little table in the local public house and the men would buy her a drink. This would infuriate Henry who would down a couple of beers and get drunk. He would then come home late and throw Alice and their daughters out into the street in their nightclothes and they would have to spend the night in a neighbour's house. Henry liked fish and ate it every day. Eventually when he died Alice, who hated the smell of fish, hurled her frying pan over the garden wall exclaiming that as long as she lived she would never cook fish again, and she never did.

c.1935

From L-R Margaret, Phyllis Henry ,Elsie, Alice, Gladys, Ida

Henry and Alice's daughters were all beautiful but of remarkably different temperament. They sang round the piano in the parlour, went to the seaside for holidays and eventually married. The parlour was decorated around the mantle-piece and over the dining table with dark red plush velvet edged with tassels and with pictures on the wall depicting the misery one could face if you took the wrong road in life.

The house in Greenwood Road still stands and during a refurbishment a letter addressed to Alice was found under the floorboards. It was from a friend in Kettering who with great sorrow gives news of the deaths of three of her relatives during the 1919 flu epidemic and tells of what a terrible blow it is to her father, just returned from the war. This letter was printed in the Northampton Chronicle & Echo and reminds us how tenuous life was in the early part of the 20th century.

Christine Whittemore   2007

Chapter 4
WORK MEMORIES AND PLACES

WORKING AT THE 'REP'

I was just five years old when I decided I wanted to make 'dresses' for the theatre.

In November 1958, at the ripe old age of fifteen, I had the chance to help make costumes for the Royal Theatre's pantomime, 'Aladdin'. I worked with Emily Tuckley, the then Wardrobe Mistress, in a room under the stage of the 'Rep'. It was a whole new world and a dream come true.

I was taken to the New Theatre at a very young age, experiencing 'variety' and 'ballet'. Then at the age of nine I started to go to the 'Rep' every week on a Monday night with my friend and our mothers. They, (our mothers) sat in the then 'Upper Circle' and my friend Ricky and I sat in the 'Gallery'. We both attended Mollie Mayhew's School of Dancing, but that is another story.

During my three and a half years at the 'Rep' I learnt my craft with lots of help from Emily Tuckley and Tom Osborne Robinson, the designer. He was instrumental in my attending the Art School to study Theatre Design with him and Life drawing and History of Costume with Henry Bird. I also studied for my City and Guilds Needlework at the Technical College and passed.

After leaving Northampton in 1961 I worked in Stratford upon Avon, Windsor, got married and produced three sons. I returned to the 'Rep' in 1977 for one play, Shakespeare's 'Twelfth Night' and again in 1978 for twenty five years, retiring in 2003.

Royal Theatre Wardrobe

I look back at my time at the 'Rep' with fond memories of meeting lots of different people, working on very different shows such as Shakespeare, Comedy, Drama, Musical and Pantomime. My job entailed not only making costumes for the next production but 'doing the washing' and repairing the costumes for the play on that night.

I loved my job and always thought that I would not want to leave but after my last four years since the merger (take over) with the Derngate Theatre in 1999 I was very happy to retire.

With the loss of our Designer, Artistic Director and Administrator to be replaced by line managers and Chief Executive without an atom of artistic ability between them the 'Rep' was a very different place and not somewhere I wanted to be.

Val Knowles 2008

MY FIRST JOB

My first job was at Modern Fittings, Northampton as a plastics fabricator. They mostly made Perspex signs and shop displays. My wage was £4.2s.6d. (£4.12 1/2p in silly money) and when I got home with my first wage-packet I asked my mum how much she wanted. I don't think she had thought about it, 'Oh, I don't know - give us a pound.' - so I did and always after that, irrespective of how much I earned, I always gave her one quarter of my wages.

There were five of us working there; including me and another young lad. The workshop was on the first floor and downstairs on the ground floor was the big circular saw and the store of complete sheets of Perspex . The cellar was full of off-cuts, which were sent off to be ground up and made into such things as buttons. Perspex can't be melted down and has to be ground up to be re-used.

Our 'bread and butter' work was making windshields for motor bikes and scooters. The windshield shape was cut out, three sheets at a time with a router. The rough, cut edges were then hand scraped with a spokeshave to smooth them, then they were stripped of the protective paper and washed. Next they were flame polished - this involved running a flame from a torch along the edge just melting it and creating a bright finish. If this was tried with an unwashed screen it would blacken and ruin the finish. The skill was in keeping the flame on for just the right length of time and keeping it moving. We lads practiced on pieces of scrap before we were let loose on the real thing. Polishing on a rotary mop was used for all other jobs. One could look *through* the piece and watch the polishing effect from the inside, so as to speak. This helped me to understand the polishing process when I took up jewellery making.

The one thing we didn't make were neon signs. Northampton in the 60s was renown for sign-makers, even exporting them abroad, I can remember we made a claw sign for a shop in Malta, but a lot of the neon signs were going to Spain, the British having just discovered it.

I had two mates who also worked for sign-makers in the town and we would go climbing in Snowdonia at the weekends. On the Friday we would change at our workplaces into our climbing gear and meet up to hitch-hike to North Wales. We would sleep out in the open (we never bothered with tents). Saturday was spent climbing and walking as was Sunday morning. We would start back Sunday afternoon and if we got back in the evening we would sleep at home, if we didn't we would go straight back to work, put on our working clothes and carry on as normal. Needless to say, we didn't do this every week!

The displays we made were mainly for jewellery shops, little stands for rings, watches &c., we also made little shelves and tubes. Most of these were simple jobs, the parts were cut out, cleaned, polished and assembled with Tensol Cement No.6 which I think was Perspex dissolved in chloroform.

I remember this bloke turning up on the shop floor with some drawings one day and stinking of perfume - not aftershave, *ladies' perfume*. 'Hello,' I thought, and kept well away from him. When he'd gone I had a chance to see the drawings he'd brought, they were for a Perspex machine guard and the name on the drawings was 'Avon Cosmetics' - that explained the perfume! Once we bought in a chunk of 'Optical Perspex' - this was more expensive than ordinary Perspex and much more transparent, I call it a chunk because it was about two or three inches thick and about eighteen by twelve inches. I heard it was for a window in some sort of device connected with nuclear reactors.

One day the other lad and myself accidentally discovered glue sniffing. We had a delivery of materials and such things as polishing compounds and cement was taken straight up to the workshop whilst the sheets went into the racks downstairs.

We went up while the invoices were signed and put the kettle on as it was almost morning break. I noticed a wet patch on one corner of a box. A cement can had sprung a leak. We used to put the cement in empty, plastic washing-up squeezy bottles to use, so we grabbed all the bottles and topped them up from the leaking can. We filled up all the bottles and ended empting a little out of one that was really on its last legs, being encrusted with old, dirty cement. We commented on what a lovely smell it had and were squeezing this bottle and sniffing the vapour coming out, passing it to each other. The next thing I remember was lying on the fire escape with my mate and feeling really queasy. I didn't eat my sandwiches that break!

Jack Plowman 2008

MY FIRST JOB
Barbour Threads Overstone Road

I was working in an office in Overstone Road during the platform sole era of the Seventies. I was never much taken with the style, and my platforms were about a third of an inch, or one centimetre if you prefer new-fangled measures. Our office junior, on the other hand, was far more adventurous, and clonked about the lino-covered floorboards like a militant Woodentop. Her platform shoes had inch and a half soles, four inch heels, and weighed as much as a box of groceries. I know. I tried them on once, and once was enough. 'Coming into land' I said, as I staggered toward my seat.

Those shoes were the talk of the office, mostly when their owner was out of earshot. One of the older typists said 'If she had to wear shoes like that, she wouldn't like it.' Having known several people whose physical conditions, such as childhood TB, condemned them to ugly dark brown surgical boots for life, I took her point - which makes me wonder if Northampton's orthopaedic bootmakers jumped on the platform bandwagon. The number of foot injuries rocketed during the craze, when girls tumbled off their own shoes, buckling ankles as they fell. Maybe local surgical bootmakers cashed-in then.

Kate Wills

NATIONAL UNION OF BOOT AND SHOE OPERATIVES
1920 – 30

I would say that 90% of Northampton 's work force were boot and shoe operatives, my father was the 'Trade-man' for his department, so I was aware from a very early age of the union's existence as they used to say 'you always took your work home with you.'

There were always signs of the Union because of Union Literature, Rule Books, Members Cards and other items in our home, so I was well aware of the Union as a school boy. I was made well aware of what the Union represented as a means of controlling working conditions for workers in the boot trade, by providing a platform for the discussion by management and the Union concerning conditions of work: management's costs, operatives' pay, and other various items that came along, so as not to interfere with the flow of the work. In other words, to prevent a strike by workers.

Perry Street

I started work at 14 years of age in 1932 at the firm of Crockett and Jones situated in Perry Street, Northampton. It was not necessary to join the Union until you were aged 16 years of age; there were no benefits between the age of 16 and 18. I think that we paid one shilling a week at 18 years of age. (present day equivalent of 5p).

The 'Northampton Union Branch' operated in two sections -:

Number one: Overstone Road.   This was the main head office for overall administration of all branch business, (both branches).

Number two: St Crispin's Hall, Earl Street. This section covered the factories for admin purposes covering the Clicking Room, Closing Room, Skin Room and Pattern Room.

Number three: This section covered every other department in the factory i.e. Making Room, Rough Stuff, Finishing Room, Basement and finally Shoe Room and Packing.

Offices came under management.

The Northampton branch did not operate what is known as

a *'Closed Shop'*, this means you were not compelled to join. This of course meant that you had no claim of union protection regarding your contract of work, which meant you operated conditions directly to the management. Firms who operated this system of conditions to management without union involvement were known as 'Sweat Shops'.

As I write I am 89 years of age and can recall that in the 1920's and 30's factory firms were referred to as *good, bad* or not *too bad*. One of the well known reasons concerned working days, this was there was virtually no full time work, only short time, which could be operated in various ways. It was mainly this factor that determined a firm's character. This came about because of the union's system of operations with its members.

The Union system was that if in any working month you could 'sign in' for three consecutive days each week, working only 3 days at your factory, the union would give you one day's pay, therefore you received a wage for 4 days work instead of three. My factory Crocket and Jones always operated this system in co-operation with the union, so was known as a good shop

Other firms operated one week on and one week off, so you would only have one week's wage to cover 2 weeks living. These were known as not too bad, only because you tried to earn a few bob doing casual work on your week off.

The third method was you would be given time-off without warning and at odd times which prevented you from signing-on for your three waiting days at your Union branch, obviously these firms were known as bad. Finally, Northampton branch to its' credit would always respect members of the unions of other industries who came to work here, giving them full branch benefits on condition they kept their own Union Card paid up.

Reg Spittles 2007

THE GREAT FIRE AT THE CO-OP

In the past, for a time, I worked at the Co-operative Wholesale Society, first at their depot in Guildhall Road

Co-op building (centre) Guildhall Road

and then when we moved, in Ardington Road in the old shoe factory. We swapped many tales over tea breaks and I learnt much about what it had been like in the Services during WWII - not all, I'm sure, entirely true!

One of my colleagues, a Welshman, told me a tale of the Co-operative Society in Abington Street.

It seems that the firemen at the then new fire station on the Mounts were cleaning their fire-engine one day when a call came that there was a fire at the Co-op, they hurriedly replaced all the gear on the machine and sped to the fire.

The route taken in those days was across the Mounts and down Newland, along the side of the Market Square and sharp left into Abington Street. When the engine reached the bottom of the Market Square the driver applied the brakes and the ladders, which someone had forgotten to strap on, continued across the street and through Burtons the Tailors' plate-glass window!

When they finally reached the Co-op they found the fire had been a small blaze in a pile of coco mats and had been extinguished by an employee with a fire-extinguisher!

Jack Plowman   2007

BROWN BROTHERS

I first started work in December 1959 as a post and filing clerk at Brown Brothers on the Bedford Road in Northampton, a large engineering company, who at that time had a few hundred employees. I was completely overwhelmed by the size of the place for the first two or three weeks, especially the noise and smells of the factory, as I had to collect and deliver post and memos to the far reaches of the site.

The offices were very old fashioned, the lighting was still very large bulbs and the lift between the four floors was a cage with folding metal doors, which was always getting stuck between floors and you would walk down the corridor and see either legs or a face and you would have to press the buttons to let them out.

After a few weeks I became part of the stock control team and part of my job was to find out the reason for discrepancies between the records and the actual stock. Having an enquiring mind, I enjoyed this. I obviously hoped there were not too many written errors, as they could have been mine.

What made it a good place to work were the people, the majority of whom were friendly and cheerful. Many of them were real characters, including one of my managers, who would stop what he was doing and whistle or sing a quick burst of opera and then carry on as normal. He also cat-napped at lunch times and a couple of times we had to go to Cow Meadow to wake him up when he did not return to work. Then there was Cyril, who chain smoked and to get the most from each cigarette, he put a pin in about $1/8^{th}$ of an inch from the end, held the pin until the cigarette had burnt right down, then lit the next one with the remains, but he did not always put them right out and we had a few wicker waste baskets go up in flames.

I thoroughly enjoyed my job and in fact went on to work for the company in many capacities for nearly twenty years, and I still have friends whom I made in my first months at Brown's and have happy memories of the people and the building, which unfortunately was demolished twenty five years ago.

Linda Kemp 2007

Chapter 5
INNS AND OUTS

PUBS OF NORTHAMPTON TOWN

The drinking house (pub, inn, tavern &c.) has been with us for a long time. It has always been natural for members of any community at times when work is over and food eaten to get together to relax and talk and if a drink is in the offering, so much the better!

In the old days when most of us lived in villages the centres of village life were the pub and the church. This continued after the Industrial Revolution when the farms became more mechanised and didn't need so many workers and the factories opened up and needed people, so there was a great migration of folk from the fields to the factories and the function of the village inn was taken over by the corner street pub.

A market town like Northampton needed inns and taverns as well as the village pub equivalent, the alehouse. The alehouse was for meeting in, drinking and perhaps eating. The tavern served the same sort of purpose, but was larger and offered accommodation, whereas the inn was a grander affair and could offer all of the above as well as stables for horses and carriages.

In the eighteenth century the Northampton Mercury often ran advertisements for inns and taverns with the information that 'market rooms' were available. These were for patrons to display their goods on market days. Usually these were samples of seeds or agricultural tools, but on occasion such things as 'menageries' were on show. Rooms would also be used on market days for such trades as periwig makers and 'rupture masters'.

Accommodation was essential as one couldn't load up your sheep or cows on a lorry and drive to market and return the same day; they would have to be driven along the roads, perhaps for several days and put up in fields outside town [Cow Meadow being one] until the market opened. This facility was so vital to the town's economy that after the Great Fire of 1675 local gentry opened their houses to serve as inns until they could be rebuilt. If this hadn't been done, the markets and fairs would have ceased and what was left of Northampton would have died and become a ghost town. Today Time Team might have come here to dig in the fields and find the 'lost town' of Northampton!

I started my drinking career when I was about sixteen, like all my contemporaries, before the legal age. However, my experiences of licensed premises goes back to when I was a young lad and my parents and I on Sundays would walk out to some distant pub with a garden and my dad would go inside and get drinks whilst my mother and I would sit outside. As my dad pointed out, I was only a boy, so could not have the man's drink of beer – I could have Tizer, cider, or the ladies' drink, lager. In those days lager only came in half pint bottles and was served in a trumpet glass with a dash of lime, just like at the end of the Film *Ice Cold in Alex*. As I sometimes had one of each, I occasionally must have gone home with a pint of snake-bite inside me!

In 1957 the last two Northampton breweries, Phipps' and Northampton Brewery Company (N.B.C.) merged to form Phipps Northampton Brewery Ltd. This meant that 711 Phipps' and 420 NBC pubs came under one management and in 1968 they were taken over and became Watney Mann (Midlands) Ltd. This meant that nearly all the pubs in the town were Watney pubs, the only exceptions that I recall were; the Bear (M&B), Garibaldi (Bass), Headlands (Charles Wells), North Star (Ansells), Saddler's Arms (Davenports) and Shipman's (Freehouse).

So I saw the demise of the variety of drink on offer from two breweries and the rise of 'Watneyland' and little to choose between the various weak beers they sold. Even so, I still enjoyed a drink, as the main purpose of going into a pub is to be sociable, not to get drunk!

In the late 1960s when I was working as a self-employed archaeologist I spent the winter working for Watney Mann and I can remember going into the Malt Shovel, opposite the brewery at Christmas. It seemed that this was the custom, at least with the North Brewery. We worked as usual up to lunchtime and then we all clocked out and trooped across the road to the pub, which stood right opposite the main gates. During this session the foremen of the various departments came over with their long boxes of pay packets, which they distributed to their men (this ritual was usually carried out during the Friday afternoon tea-break in the canteen). Having handed out the pay, each foreman was then expected to stand his lads a pint. I had noticed that whilst we were being paid, the landlord was pulling scores of pints of 'S.P.A.' so this must have been a regular custom. The pub was much smaller than it is now, as the back has been opened up and the front is no longer two bars, so it was a very crowded, but jovial atmosphere on that day - especially after a pint or two. The foremen had a pint with us and left. Suddenly someone called, 'It's time!' and we all trooped over the road, queued up to clock-on and, I assumed, prepared to return to work, but instead of going into the building we all turned about, marched out of the other end of the clock-house and returned to our pints left in the pub.

The Brewery had recently employed a new gate-man, resplendent in his uniform with his medal ribbons from World War II. He was a true 'old soldier' and tried to stop us – all to no avail and although exhorted by many of us to desert his post and join us for a Christmas drink, he steadfastly refused. That is probably why the Brewery gave him the job!

In the afternoon there was a raffle and all the staff were there. Phipps-Walker who I had never seen before, conducted the draw. From the comments about him from the men around me, I concluded that he was a very popular and respected man. The prizes varied, from whole hampers, cases of a half-dozen bottles of assorted spirits, turkeys and crates of bottled beer. There were no tatty prizes, and it was fixed – insomuch as everyone won *something* – I won a crate of a dozen pint bottles of Jumbo Stout, most of which my dad drank! The Brewery might have been owned by Watneys then, but the old spirit that must have been around for years still clung on.

Of course, the old Brewery has now gone and Carlsberg now occupies the site. ***What's Brewing,*** the CAMRA paper described the Malt Shovel in June 1999 thus: - *A Free house which stands at the real ale lovers idea of the Gates of Hell...Carlsberg fizz-factory.*

In the early 1970s my wife and I bought a house in Vernon Street almost opposite the Grandby Arms, a typical 19th century street corner pub and it became our local.

It had its regulars; in fact, it had little more and needed no more as I cannot recall it ever being empty. It was a small place and started life in the 19th century as a beer-shop. It has all the characteristics (and characters!) associated with the old 'Home from Home' local. The atmosphere, especially on a cold night, was warm and welcoming. There were seats that were 'somebody's' – and although no one minded you sitting in them, when 'somebody' came in you were expected to give them up. Every night there were the same faces and all the local gossip was aired.

We had draconian licensing laws in those days, so on Sundays (Noon-2pm.) we would take our jug and get it filled just before closing time, to return home having had a couple of hours in the Granby while the Sunday joint was cooking over the road – Happy Days! After a couple of years or so we were compulsorily purchased, the area flattened, and redeveloped.

It may appear that I have eulogised over a small back street pub, but *this* pub was in my personal sphere of experience and I am well aware that all over Northampton - indeed all over England - there were thousands of such pubs like this one, pubs that sold most of their beer to perhaps 30 to 50 families within a couple of streets of the place. They were the backbone of English pubs and drinking and sadly, at least in the south, largely gone for ever, as have the communities that they served.

Jack Plowman   2007

NORTHAMPTON BREWERIES

Records of breweries in the early days of Northampton are very sparse and originally inns and taverns would have brewed their own ale on the premises. Large houses and estates also brewed their own for their employees, part of their wages being paid in beer. In the past potable drinking water was almost unknown and the safe drink was beer. Part of the process of making ale and beer involves boiling the water so any germs would be killed and the yeast that was added later would not tolerate any new ones that turned up.

Pickering Phipps

Reliable records begin in the 19th century. Seven breweries appeared between 1817 and 1900 and eventually were taken over one at a time until there was by 1957 only one, ***Phipps Northampton Brewery Ltd.***

The first was *Phipps Brewery*, started by Pickering Phipps at Towcester in 1801. In 1817 he established a brewery in this town on the west side of Bridge Street. An ideal site with water and road access. Breweries use copious amounts of water [called *liquor*] not just for making the beer, but for washing vessels, cleaning and cooling the brew.

In 1856 the *Phoenix Brewery* opened on Bridge Street to the north of Phipps' brewery. Confusingly this was started by the Phillips brothers. Around 1870 it was calling itself *The Steam Brewery* and by 1874 it was known as *The Northampton Brewery Company (Late Phillips Brothers), Northampton and Burton-On-Trent* later still the *Northampton Brewery Company* or *N.B.C.*

In 1864 Thomas Ratcliffe established a brewery in Commercial Street and this became known as the *Albion Steam Brewery*, it expanded and became just the *Albion Brewery* it was acquired by *Phipps & Co.* in 1899.

Around 1864 the *Lion Brewery* appeared on the east side of Bridge Street between the river and South Bridge Road. It was acquired by *Northampton Brewery Company* in 1890.

T. Manning & Co. were at the *Castle Brewery* by 1885. This was on Black Lion Hill and I understand it was from this establishment that the reliquary slab of St. Ragener was recovered and returned to St. Peter's Church when the brewery was demolished. It was acquired by *P. Phipps & Co. Ltd.* in 1933.

Youil Bros. & Co. were brewing in the Kettering Road in 1870 to circa 1890. Sometime around 1894 *Major-Lucas & Co.* were brewing and by 1903 Walker and Soames were the brewers at the *Victoria Brewery.*

The last to appear was the *Abington Brewery* in about 1900 between the Lutterworth and Wycliffe Roads on the Wellingborough Road. It was first known as the *Abington Park Brewery* but by 1914 it was called the *Abington Brewery Co. Charles Wells Ltd.* acquired it in 1963 to get its pubs and shortly afterwards they demolished the brewery buildings.

Time line:
1817 Phipps Brewery.
1856 Phoenix Brewery.
1864 Albion Brewery.
c.1864 Lion Brewery.
1874 Phoenix Brewery becomes Northampton Brewery Co.
1885 Castle Brewery.
1890 Northampton Brewery Co. Acquires the Lion Brewery.
c. 1890 Victoria Brewery.
1899 Phipps Brewery acquires the Albion Brewery.
c. 1900 Abington Brewery.
1933 Phipps Brewery acquires Castle Brewery.
c. 1933 Victoria Brewery ceases trading.
1957 Amalgamation of Phipps and Northampton Brewery Co.
1960 Amalgamation of above taken over by Watney Mann.
1963 Charles Wells acquire Abington Brewery and demolish it.
1973 Carlsberg began brewing in their new brewery on the site of the amalgamation of Phipps and Northampton Brewery Co.

Flood outside North Brewery

Much of this information came from:-
Breweries in Northamptonshire,
A survey by Geoffrey H. Starmer.
Bulletin of Industrial Archaeology,
CBA Group 9, No. 14, Oct.1970.

Jack Plowman   2008

Chapter 6
SPORTS, RECREATION AND
OPEN SPACES

A BRIEF HISTORY OF NORTHAMPTON TOWN
F.C.

On 6th March 1897 a meeting was held at the Princess Royal on the Wellingborough Road, and from that gathering Northampton Town F.C. was born.

The County Ground was obtained, with the proviso that the games did not start until September 1st, and ended by May 1st.

Application was made, and accepted, to join the Northants League (currently known as the United Counties League) and three professionals were signed on a part-time basis. The rest of the players were made up of enthusiastic amateurs.

The first game played at the County Ground was a friendly against Earls Barton. Northampton won 4-1.

The first league game ended in a 2-0 defeat at Desborough, and the second a 4-1 reverse to Rushden. However, the first league match at home gave the club its first victory, 3-1, also against Rushden.

Northampton Town finished 4th in the league and lost £54 on the season, but overall not a bad start.

The 1898/99 season was one to remember, Northampton Town won the Northants League, gaining 28 out of a possible 32 points. Only one game was lost, and it was decided to join the Midland League for the

1899/1900 season, with a higher standard of play, and the club making over £200 profit.

Northampton finished 3rd twice in the Midland League and applied to join the Southern League for the 1901/02 season. The team was now all professional players. Northampton finished 11th out of sixteen teams, not a bad result for the club's first season in this league.

The F.A. Cup brought the most interest reaching round one for the first time, losing at home 2-0 to Sheffield United in front of 15,000 fans.

After several mid table finishes, Northampton Town finished bottom of the Southern League 1905/06 and again 1906/07.

Herbert Chapman was appointed the first manager of the 'Cobblers' in April 1907. An immediate improvement was made and a league finish of 8th followed and in 1908/09 Northampton became champions of the Southern League.

After beating Plymouth 2-1 in the last game of the season, Northampton Town were invited to meet Newcastle at Stamford Bridge to compete for the Charity Shield. In those days competed for by the Football League champions and the Southern League champions. Newcastle won 2-0.

Under Chapman Northampton finished 4th, 2nd, and 3rd in the league and beating Sheffield Wednesday before losing to Nottingham Forest in the F.A. Cup.

Herbert Chapman left the Cobblers in May 1912 to manage Leeds, Huddersfield and Arsenal and won 4 league championships, 2 runners-up and 2 F.A. Cup winners.

On 21st October 1911 the Cobblers signed Walter Tull from Tottenham Hotspur. Walter was the first black professional footballer to play in England, and a memorial outside Sixfields Stadium on Walter Tull Way commemorates this.

In 1920 the old Southern League became the Third Division South of the Football League.

Northampton Town Footballers 1920's

With only the champions being promoted, Northampton Town played in the Third Division South from 1920 to 1958. They finished 2nd on two occasions (1927/8 and 1949/50)

During the war years 1939/45 Northampton Town played in a midland section of a wartime league and

Bill Shankly played nine times for the Cobblers. League football was suspended.

On 4th January 1958 Northampton Town played Arsenal at home in the third round of the F.A. Cup. Northampton won 3-1 in front of an all-ticket 21,344 crowd. They lost in the next round at Liverpool by the same score, watched by 56,939 fans.

In 1958/59 the Fourth Division was added to the Football League, being made up of the teams that finished in the bottom half of the Third Division South and North Leagues respectively. Northampton (13th) became a Fourth Division Club.

In 1959 Dave Bowen (Arsenal's captain that lost to the Cobblers) became Northampton Town's new manager.

From 1961 to 1969 the Cobblers were promoted from the Fourth Division to the First Division and back to the Fourth, the first team to do this and I believe still the quickest.

3rd in Division Four (1960/61) followed by champions of the Third Division (1962/63), runners-up to Newcastle in the Second Division (1964/65).

The home game against Fulham on 23rd April 1966 was watched by a record crowd of 24,523. Fulham won 4-2.

Joe Mercer, manager of Manchester City, said 'The miracle of 1966 was not England winning the World Cup, but Northampton Town reaching Division One.'

On 7th February 1970 the Cobblers played Manchester United at home in the 5th round of the F.A.

Cup. Manchester United won 8-2, George Best scoring six of the goals.

In 1975/76 the Cobblers finished 2nd in Division 4 and were promoted. Bill Dodein was manager. Alas they were relegated back to the Fourth Division 1976/77 and ten miserable years followed and in 1985 they had to seek re-election to the League after finishing 23rd in Division Four.

Graham Carr was appointed manager for the 1985/86 season and a very respectable 8th was followed by Champions of Division Four 1986/87. After finishing 6th in Division 3 (1987/88) Graham Carr was forced to sell his better players to help balance the books. Northampton Town found themselves back in Division Four 1990/91 and Graham Carr resigned and joined Blackpool.

The Cobblers were put up for sale and the infamous Michael McRitchie became chairman. Under McRitchie the club finances got even worse and the club was put into administration 1992/93 season. The Cobblers finished bottom of the league in 1993/94 and had to seek re-election for the second time.

On 15th October 1994 the Cobblers played the first home game against Barnet at their new Sixfields Stadium. It was a 1-1 draw, with Martin Aldridge scoring the first goal at Sixfields.

In January 1995 Ian Atkins became manager and guided the club to two play-off finals at Wembley –

1997 Swansea won 1-0 and promotion to Division 2.

1998 Grimsby lost 1-0

Divisions 1 – 2 – 3 – 4 have been replaced by the Premier League, the Championship League, Division One and Division Two.

Northampton Town are at present in Division One. The current manager is Stuart Gray.

Duncan Bolton 2008

Northampton Town Football Club 1959 - 1966 (Life on the Ground Staff)

I first played football for St George's Primary School aged 7 years, where, if I remember correctly, we had little success. Many of us young boys would go to the local park and play football until it was too dark to see the ball.

Campbell Square School FC Champions of the Football League 1958-59

On leaving St George's I moved to Campbell Square Secondary School and joined the Intermediate team there, we settled into a good side. The end of the season found us at the top of the league without having lost a single game. This success was due to the dedication and determination of the players, but equally to the marvellous help and encouragement by the sports masters John Howland and Gwyn Morteca. We were hardy players, our arc rivals being John Claire School team where we would kick lumps out of each other to get a favourable result. You had to be hard to go to Campbell Square School, it was almost a place of survival. The masters were wonderful to the boys, very sympathetic to the backgrounds and disadvantages that many of the pupils had to face. The teachers worked miracles from the school's poor catchment area, and encouraged anyone willing to learn whether it be science or football.

I left school and started my working life as a pattern cutter in the shoe trade attending the Technical College in St George's Avenue. During this time I was invited for trials at the County Ground and was asked if I would like to join the ground staff. Of course I jumped at the idea of a footballing career.

My duties along with the other ground-staff boys were to sweep the terraces and stands after each game, clean the senior player's boots and run errands. I remember cleaning the toilets, which were infested with rats, John Linnell, another ground-staff lad would be waiting outside with a shovel to kill them as they tried to escape. Other jobs involved making sure that the match kit was complete and ready for the forthcoming game, plus cleaning out the large communal bath and showers after each match. This was the norm at all football clubs at this time, it sounds rather dreary, but we had a fabulous time, full of pranks and laughter and were treated really well by the senior footballer players. I also improved my game immensely by training daily with the professional players, being coached by the manager Dave Bowen, and coaches Joe Payne and Jack Jennings.

On Saturdays I would play in the 'B' team, but after a while I was promoted to the 'A' team under the guidance of two old 'Cobblers', Freddie Ramscar and Bill Barron.

After playing in the County Youth Team I was selected to play for England Youth against Scotland. As you can imagine this was my proudest moment. This was excelled a few weeks later when I was invited into the manager's office to be told that I had been selected again, but this time I was to captain the side. With the England team I played in Rumania, Israel and Ireland gaining eight 'caps' and many happy memories.

On my return from Israel I signed professional papers for the 'Cobblers' and then I realised that pro-football is not all glamour. One had to work very hard to be at all successful. Pre season training was incredibly hard, we would run for miles relentlessly, following this our legs felt like lead with every part of our body aching, then out would come the 'Deep Heat' followed by a massage and we would be ready for the next session.

Strict discipline had to be kept, no drinking or socialising after Wednesday nights, always of smart appearance, shirt and tie, suit or sports jacket worn daily was the norm. We were in awe of the manager and trainers, we slept, ate and drank football. Also I was shown a different world, I stayed in hotels, this was unheard of with boys of my background, I travelled, used airports and visited different countries, I experienced different food and saw how other people lived. Whilst in Rumania, I remember the team living on bread and jam for days the food being so awful, until the manager eventually found eggs for us. I also learnt how to play cards, like today this was popular on the coach going to away games.

Northampton Town Team Photo 1962
Royal Daring F.C. Belgium

I was with the 'Cobblers' during the climb to the first division before moving to Brentford. I had two seasons playing for this London club before being invited to play in Belgium along with two other English players; I suppose we were the pioneers of English players joining foreign clubs. I played for a club named 'Royal Daring' in Brussels, and then moved to Bruges. I spent three happy years in Belgium the football there was excellent, most players were part time at this time and we played the fixtures on Sunday, unheard of in this country in the late sixties. Whilst in Belgium I played in the UEFA cup against teams like Feyenoord,Strausburg, Lausanne and many more famous clubs, travelling all over Europe.

On my return to England I played part time, becoming player/manager at Corby, then joining Wellingborough and Bedford finishing in my forties playing for the 'Chenicks' at the ON's sports ground. Whilst playing part time I concentrated on my life after football. I learnt by starting in sales the fundamental elements of business until I eventually started a company of my own manufacturing heavy-duty illustrated, printed polythene sacks. I get satisfaction when I visit places like garden centres and see my sacks with artwork that we have created to show the various materials inside, but nothing will ever excel the rush of running out onto the football pitch at the start of a game, especially under floodlights, hearing the supporter's cheers, with the smell of the various potions and creams clinging to injured limbs and sore muscles.

Football played well, is and will always be the beautiful game.

Brian Etheridge   2007

BOWLING CLUBS IN NORTHAMPTON

A bowls club opened in Abington Park in July 1904, it was opened as a public Green at a charge of two pence per hour per person. The cost of hiring the entire rink was two shillings and sixpence for the first hour, and one shilling and sixpence for each hour after, but you had to book twenty-four hours in advance.

Nowadays, there are several clubs that play regularly in the park, they are Abington Park Rangers and the Wanderers.

As well as those two clubs, and the general public, many clubs connected to factories and other businesses in the town forming the league called the Abington Park League also use the greens.

Over 60's Bowling Club with the Abington Park Museum in the background.

The County Ground Club, Kingsthorpe and West End plus the two clubs mentioned above and many others, are all members of the Northampton Bowling Association, and compete each year for the Manfield Cup which was presented by Mr. Manfield, M.P. and Mr. Jas. Manfield, J.P.

There are also several other private and public greens in Northampton.

Doreen Batchelor 2008

COGENHOE BOWLS CLUB

Cogenhoe Bowls Club began as an indoor bowling club in September 1985 with 30+ members who played in the Working Men's Club. There was soon talk of opening an outdoor bowls club in the village, and by September 1986 two members discussed the possibility of creating a six rink green on the playing fields in Cogenhoe, but it was decided there was not enough land and they had to look for another site.

Adjacent to the lower school in Brafield Road was a piece of land owned by the Marquis of Northampton. He gave permission for the club to rent it for £150 per acre, but the club was able to negotiate for 0.8 of an acre, and work commenced in March 1987.

The base of the green is made up of 15-20 mms of aggregate, then pea gravel and finally a binding layer of sharp sand. We then had to mix our own soil with a special sand. Samples of soil had already been sent to Aberystwyth University for advice as to whether it could be used with the sand.

During the main school holidays we enlisted the help of the village lads and others to help lay the sand and soil, and then to tread it firm. The treading was done five times to make it firm and level, with everyone assembled making little shuffling steps to pad it down. The turf was then laid in a brick fashion, enough to make the six rinks. It has been said that as the lads from the village helped with the laying of the green there was no vandalism.

The first match was played in May 1988, at the start of the outdoor season. The pavilion was constructed in 1989.

Doreen Batchelor

Doreen Batchelor is a member of the Cogenhoe Bowls Club and Northampton Heritage Hunters group. Along with other members of the group, Doreen is researching material for their Northampton's People & Places project, her special interest being the history of bowls in the town. She welcomes any information fellow members of NALH have on this subject.

CINEMAS AND THEATRES

1884 Royal Theatre and Opera House – Guildhall Rd

1888 Temperance Hall – Newland
        Headquarters of Temperance Society

1901 Palace of Varieties Music Hall –bottom of Gold St

1908 Temperance Hall - became a cinema

1910 County Electric Pavillion Cinema – Gold St
        Lasted only 11 years and showed only silent
        pictures.

1911 Cinema de Luxe – Campbell St

1912 Palace of Varieties Music Hall – Gold St
        Changed to a "Picture Palace" – Gold St

1912 East Park Picturedrome – Kettering Rd
First purpose built cinema in town

1912 New Theatre – Abington St
(locally called the Hippodrome)

1913 Vint's Palace – Gold St
It showed both films and variety acts

1919 Majestic Cinema – Gold St
Replaced Vint's Palace – Gold St

1920 Corn Exchange – Market Square
Converted into the Exchange Cinema

1920 Vaudeville Electric Cinema – Grove Rd

1922 Salon de Dance – Weedon Rd
Replaced the Victory Hall – Weedon Rd

1929 Exchange Cinema screened town's first "talkie"
"The Singing Fool" by Al Jolson

1929 Vaudeville Electric Cinema closed

1930 Regal Super Cinema – Grove Rd
(formerly the Vaudeville Electric Cinema)

1936 <u>Savoy Cinema</u> – Abington Square
(later the ABC Cinema)

1936 <u>Electric Cinema</u> – St. James
Changed name to <u>Roxy</u>

1937 <u>Majestic Cinema</u> – closed

1947 <u>Roxy Cinema</u> closed, became part of Dove's cycle
Accessories factory

1950 <u>Exchange Cinema</u> changed name to <u>The Gaumont</u>

1956 <u>Cinema de Luxe</u> closed

1956 <u>Regal Super Cinema</u> changed name to <u>Essoldo</u>

1957 Coliseum and Picturedrome closed

1958 New Theatre closed (demolished 1960)

1960 Tivoli Cinema closed

1962 Ritz Cinema closed

1963 Temperance Hall closed, the oldest cinema in
      Britain, and became a Bingo Hall.

1964 Gaumont changed name to Odeon

1968 Essoldo closed, became a Bingo Hall

1974 Odeon closed, converted to Bingo Hall

1983 Derngate Theatre – Guildhall Rd
      (next to the Royal Theatre)

1995 ABC Cinema closed

1999 Royal Theatre "merged" (or was it a takeover)
      With Derngate.

There was a cinema at the corner of College Street called The
Queen's.

The Gem cinema in Washngton Street, Kingsthorpe, showed
silent films and had a male pianist accompanying the films.
When "talkies" arrived the Gem cinema closed down.

The cinema near to Dover's factory was called The Rink and had a tin roof.

The Prince of Wales cinema on Wellingborough Road became the Plaza.

Prior to the opening of cinemas, a lot of magic lantern shows were given around St. Katherine's Street. These were mostly connected to churches.

Ivor Novello appeared at the New Theatre in a play called The Cat and the Canary.

NORTHAMPTON PARKS

As a young child I remember going for Sunday evening walks with my mum and dad during the summer along the tow path from South Bridge to Cow Meadow (now Beckett's Park).

South Bridge.   Northampton.

We used to walk right along by the river to Nunn Mills and back home through the fields, coming out into Far Cotton along Ransome Road.

Sometimes I used to walk along the same route with my friends. We used to go fishing with our bandy nets and I remember we used to go over the little bridge over the river and there was a lake with a pathway all round it. There were some concrete steps in places leading down to the main river and water used to run down these into the river. I suppose they were overflows and we used to paddle in these and I remember one day falling over in one and nearly going down into the river, but just managed to scramble out. I went home absolutely drenched. There used to be an outdoor swimming pool farther along in Midsummer Meadow and many a happy day of the school holidays was spent there. There was often a circus or a fair along this part of the meadow.

We often went for a walk up through the spinney at the edge of Delapre Abbey, up to Queen Eleanor's Cross. There was a farm next to Delapre Abbey called Home Farm, which was run by Mr. and Mrs. Wreford and there were two cottages at the side of the dairy in which farm workers lived. I lived in St. Leonard's Road at the time and next door to us was the Brown family, and Albert, their eldest son, worked on this farm. In April 1945 a Lancaster bomber with a crew of seven crashed in a field and burst into flames where Albert was ploughing with a Mr. Richardson, who lived in one of the cottages, and between them they rescued two of the crew from the blazing aircraft. They were joined by other farm workers from another farm and dragged out the other occupants, four were already dead and one died almost immediately. Mr. Albert Brown and Mr. Richardson were awarded the British Empire Medal for their bravery.

From the age of 10, I moved to Abington and my leisure time was then spent at Abington Park and the Racecourse. Usually I had charge of my little brother, who was 8 years younger than I, and the two of us set off every day, both mornings and afternoons, me pushing him in his pushchair to one of the parks, sometimes joined by friends. We had some great times, which ranged from paying 3d for a boat on Abington Park lake, to taking a clothes horse and some blankets with us to make a tent. I remember I was once so engrossed in the tent making on the Racecourse, that my brother wandered off and I spent two hours looking for him before going home to tell my mother I had lost him. The police were informed and he was found safe and well crossing backwards and forwards across the main Kettering Road.

The Boat House Beckett's Park

I suppose the most memorable times spent in a park were in Beckett's Park as a teenager, when I was a Sea Ranger, and we had our own large rowing boat named SRS Ajax, which was kept at the boat house near the locks at Beckett's Park. The boat was rowed by four oarsmen and we had a coxswain on the tiller and we used to row up the river towards what is the wide part of the River Nene, over which now runs the dual carriageway of the A45 near Brackmills.

Mavis Cook 2008

NORTHAMPTON RACECOURSE AND PADDY'S MEADOW

I was born in Semilong in 1944 and when old enough used the Racecourse as my garden and playground.

Northcote St. Urchins1946

As most of my mates came from similar homes, money being tight, fathers adjusting to family life following the war, some finding it very difficult, mothers loosing some of the freedom that came with their men folk being away, had to settle down to

114

family life. Surprising enough, this caused resentment in some homes, so the ideal place to escape to was the Racecourse which was full of adventure, open space, abandoned army barracks, swings, a slide and a roundabout that whizzed round at 50 miles an hour or so it seemed, friends and sport.

My parents both worked leaving home around 7.00 am each morning returning again around 5.30pm. There were no school clubs or organisations to look after us children so most of us from the vicinity congregated on the Racecourse. We were mostly a rag tag bunch of boys, we had and expected very little. There was always someone's mother to run to in case of need.

Here we played every ball game imaginable; we all became our own heroes. None of us had suitable footwear, mostly plimsolls in the summer and school shoes or boots in the winter. I can still remember the day that I had my first pair of football boots, these were cherished and cleaned and polished every day and were never off my feet. Despite the lack of kit and coaching many a talented sport person learnt all their skills on the Racecourse some progressing to become professionals in their chosen sport

We would arrive and play whatever sport was in season. Trees could either be stumps or football posts, coats and sweaters likewise. We would befriend the lucky boy who owned a ball and would then play for hours, only to stop for dinner as we called the mid day meal, I would charge to an aunt's house in Adelaide Street and eat a lunch of steamed suet puddings sometimes filled with onions and bacon other times apples depending on the order of the meal. I was very fortunate as my uncle was a cook in the army and knew how to make a meal out of anything available, once eaten back to the Racecourse.

Apart from the endless sport, we played in the deserted army barracks crawling through broken windows, climbing down drains, playing hide and seek. Once running across a roof I slipped and ended up with a nail slicing my head open but once stitched at the hospital returned to the same spot and continued the same game. Like most children we were oblivious of danger, when I think back it makes me realise how fearless we were.

Us Semilong boys had street rivals and often there would be a fight, for example Northcote Street against Salisbury Street, lead by their leader Hughie Hamilton. During these fights only fists were used, never feet or weapons, we would never dare tell tales to our parents as this could lead to being clipped around the ear by them for fighting in the first place.

Northcote St. Annual Day trip to Margate 1956

Later to the Racecourse came the roller skating rink, this came about in my early teenage years, it was quite the place to meet girls and show off our skills whilst skating to pop music. Here with our DA haircuts, shoe string ties and drainpipe trousers we really thought that we were irresistible.

Another memory is playing down Paddy's Meadow. This had the advantage of a river, and water is always an attraction to boys, we tried to make dams, walked the plank, fished for sticklebacks. I remember perhaps the most frightening of our games was to crawl underneath a narrow gap under the railway bridge and lay on our backs whilst the trains rattled and sped inches above us. You had to be brave to do this but even the most timid eventually got up the courage so as to become part of the gang. We were covered in coal dust when we crawled out, I remember breathing fresh air and the relief of being above ground again.

Happy days.

Brian Etheridge 2007

BRADLAUGH FIELDS – on the old golf course, Lack's Farm, Moulton Park.

Memories of 1937 – 45 as a child playing in the above areas.

The golf course was very well used and I recall watching a champion golfer playing there around 1940. It was Henry Cotton a player with only one arm, yet he was a champion.

To approach the golf course from St. David's estate we had a couple of fields to cross, a deep valley between them with a sparkling stream coming from a spring from which we drank . (This valley is now filled in with three storey flats on the site.) The second field, cattle from Lack's Farm used to graze on and the army dug several trenches on it, in which we played soldiers.

You then came to the lane up to the farm with both golf courses, Kingsthorpe and Kingsley, either side. To the left were the old, in those days ruined, farm buildings of Kingsthorpe Grange. On the golf course we used to get little button mushrooms around that area.

To the right, following the track, was Lack's Farm with the cattle sheds open. Passing the farm one came to Holton's bungalow with its woodyard at the side. (I worked there as a boy of ten or twelve making firewood bundles.) From here on the track crossed the golf course onto Holton's Lane leading to Kettering Road, passing the old Corona soft drinks factory. It housed Italian P.O.W's during the war. Ennerdale Close sheltered bungalows now stand on the site.

When you got to the base of the steep hill, which went up to Moulton Park (St. Andrew's Mental Home) you came to the large field, now a sports field. In this field was quite a large pond with, I recall, very large dragonflies in the summer. The hedges and fields were full of flowers and birds that you no longer see, i.e. skylarks, yellowhammers, finches etc. cornflowers, scarlet pimpernel, such large buttercups, moon daises.

Passing through this field we went into what is now the nature reserve. Then it was a field of trenches known as the love field, perhaps nature wasn't so reserved then.

We then get to the lane at the top of the hill, which connects Boughton Green Road with Kettering Road, via Holton's Lane.

On the other side of this lane were the lime kiln quarries, about twenty feet deep with pools of water in the bottom and loads of newts. We had great fun climbing the sides of the quarry and scrumping fruit from the orchard of the St. Andrew's Home.

Around 1942 I got caught conkering in the field near the lime kiln, the rear of today's University. I had the farmer's punishment, a whack across the behind. My mother came after my brother had run home and she kicked the farmer all over the field and she was only five foot four. Those trees are still there to remind me of that day so long ago. I still cycle past there today.

Tony Mallard 2007

THORNTON PARK, NORTHAMPTON

Thornton Park is situated in the district of Queen's Park - hence the royal street names, Clarence Avenue, Stanhope Road, Balfour Road and Queen's Park Parade to namefew. I lived in this area as a child and being the local park I spent much of my childhood there.

Thornton Park

I attended the 'Grace Wootton School of Dancing', who every summer held a dancing display there; this dance extravaganza was performed through rain and shine outside the hall on the front lawn which acted as the stage. This was a popular event and spectators would sit in front of the haw haw, many bringing deck chairs, blankets and picnics.

Dancing Girl 1950

I remember the sunken rose garden, where for some reason we had to be very quiet, could not run and would never dare to tread onto the manicured lawn. We lived in terror of the park keeper Mr.Tapp, or 'parkie' as we called him, he seemed to appear from nowhere, never dare we ride our bikes in the park, as this was forbidden, such was his authority, we never dared answer him back. We spent much of our time hiding from him, this was difficult as he and his family lived in one of the two cottages just inside the park gates.

Kingsthorpe Grove Junior Sports Day1953

I attended Kingsthorpe Grove School, this park being local to the school was used for various school activities, but perhaps the most important was Sports Day. We would trail from the school dragging all sorts of apparatus, skipping ropes, balls, sacks, eggs and spoons for the races, even bicycles for the 'slow bicycle race', all bedecked in our school team colours, we were very proud and competitive.

My friends and I would walk home from school through the park and in the autumn collect beech and chestnuts. Our Brownie and Girl Guide packs would use the park for outside activities, it was always well maintained with many flower beds and trees and a play area containing swings, a slide and and a roundabout.

Receiving our Coronation Mugs 1953

We assembled in the park to receive our Coronation mugs
following Queen Elizabeth's Coronation, these mugs seemed
to be made of Pyrex, not at all delicate or ornate,
but at the time very precious to us.

Later the hall was used as an annex for the school, being so young we were unaware of the beauty of this building although I can remember the splendid staircase, sadly even at this time in the late 1950s, the hall was falling into disrepair.

Thornton Park in later years was used by the community, it held a weekly welfare clinic, a place to take your babies to get them weighed and to check on their well being, also a place to buy cheap orange juice, formula milk and Marmite.

The hall also became a venue for wedding receptions even in its fallen splendour the gardens were ideal for wedding photos. It still has the most the wonderful cedar tree that stands at the entrance to the rose garden opposite the hall.

Thornton Park was very well used, it was popular with the neighbourhood, families would walk, picnic and socialise there. It was also a short cut from Kingsthorpe and the Kingsley areas to Dallington, Kingsheath and Kingsthorpe village and the 'King Billy' which still stands on the village green, the only disadvantage to this route was that the gate giving access to Mill Lane would be locked at night forcing late comers to walk all around the walls to Kingsthorpe Road.

Once it had a very high wall built around it's perimeter, inside this was a wooded area, great for hide and seek and courting couples, sadly this is no longer there and the wall halved in height.

Pauline Etheridge   2007

MOULTON PARK

In 1953, when I was living in Overstone and travelled into Northampton to work daily by United Counties bus, we used to pass lovely green fields opposite Manfield Hospital. At that time I could not envisage what would become of those fields, or that I would actually be living there, because of course this is where the Parklands Estate was built on land that was part of the original Moulton Park.

When I first moved into Coppice Drive (in 1960) the land at the back of the house was farmland and we often had cows looking over the fence into our garden. I remember once animals got into our garden when they got through a hole in the hedge. This was before Moulton Park Industrial Estate was established. We still have trees and fields between us and the industrial estate and to the right there are now allotments.

In Saxon times Moulton Park was known as Multune – meaning "mul" for mule and "tun" for farm. It was also known as The Kings Park and was enclosed by a high stone wall. Deer were kept there and in the 12th century hunting frequently took place by the Angevin Kings when they were visiting Northampton Castle, particularly by John (1167-1216). Richard II was also known to have stayed several days in the Royal Hunting Lodge in the park in 1381. A large mansion was built in 1572 for Sir Christopher Hatton in Moulton Park. Hatton, born at Holdenby, was Chancellor to Elizabeth I from 1587-1591. This mansion was demolished in 1861.

In 1879 the governors of St. Andrew's Hospital purchased 453 acres of farmland at Moulton Park, including a farm of 410 acres and a modest sized country house. In 1882 the farmhouse was made into a residence for patients of the hospital. There was shelter for 50 cows, a new dairy, a dairyman's cottage and piggeries. A large orchard and kitchen garden of nearly 20 acres was laid out. By 1883 it was able to supply all vegetables and fruit required by St.

Andrew's Hospital. By 1959 it was decided it was no longer economical to grow vegetables and the kitchen gardens were put down to grass. The land was gradually sold off to Northampton Borough Council and Northampton Development Corporation.

Mavis Cook 2006

Notes taken from Moulton Memories by Michael Merriman. 942.55 And booklet St. Andrew's Hospital 362.2109, both in Northampton Library Local Studies.

ABINGTON PARK

Many historical facts have been written concerning Abington Park. This version tells about the magic of growing up with the park as a garden to play in. It's the story of a 3 in 1 park. First Park houses the museum, which was always entered with baited breath, the smell of dust and polish and the sound of squeaky floor boards, as you moved from room to room, enhanced the feeling of awe. After all, who could forget the stuffed albatross suspended from the ceiling, in a room full of dioramas, with snake versus mongoose forever frozen in battle.

The Bandstand Abington Park

Of course we mustn't forget the bandstand, which featured some pretty good brass bands on sunny summer evenings. It was a place to meet perhaps a future partner. The parade around the stand was strictly adhered to, girls clockwise, boys anticlockwise, only the brave dared to walk in the wrong direction.

Adjacent to the bandstand there is a very large mound of earth, trodden smooth by generations of kid's feet to and from school. Now I have it on good authority that beneath that mound is buried a First World War army tank. I know this to be true because my school friend (age 8 ½) told me so!

Second Park is given over to swings and roundabouts and there was a uniformed attendant always on duty. He was the proud tenant of a small wooden hut on site, which enabled him to have his flask of tea and sandwiches, whilst still keeping a beady eye on all and sundry. It must be said that he did a sterling job for any unfortunate little person who fell off the equipment.

The boating lake was also part of the second park, which was a bit of a misnomer really, as it consisted of half a dozen small flat-bottomed paddle boats, and if you dangled your legs over the side it enabled you to put your feet almost on the bottom of the lake. Bandy nets and jam jars with string were the tools for catching tiddlers in the big lake. Any left over bait was fed to the swans and moorhens.

Third Park, now this was very different. You had to pass through a small wood to reach your goal and there was an element of mystery along the way. No activity in this park, so things were always tranquil. The wooded area boasted a babbling brook and a small bridge where you could stop for a while and let your imagination take over.

Of course, in reality there is only one Abington Park, a place where everyone can conditionally walk their dogs, play footie, cricket, bowls, have a cup of tea, or just browse around. What more could anyone wish for?

J.R. 2008

Chapter 7
WATERMILLS AND WATERWAYS

THE RIVER NENE - A SHORT HISTORY
FROM SOURCE TO SEA

The river Nene (Nen) rises in two places. The major tributary rises at Arbury Hill near Badby and a smaller tributary rises near Naseby and flows to Northampton to join the major source near South Bridge, and then flows to meet the sea at the Wash, a total length of 91 miles.

The Nene has always been a trade route since the Romans, who cut a channel called Cardyke from Peterborough to the river Witham at Lincoln.

The Saxons used the river for expansion, as can be seen by the many villages and churches of Saxon origin which are found along the river's route.

During the medieval period, the river was mainly used for local trade and milling and the stone from the quarries at Barnack were moved by river to build Ely and Norwich Cathedrals, among other buildings.

The first attempt to make the river more accessible to trade from the Fens was in 1728, when a channel was cut from near the 'Dog in a Doublet' east of Peterborough to Guyhirn. The original meandering river still flows through Whittlesey, Ramsey and March.

In 1871 the river eastwards from Northampton was improved by building locks which bypassed the weirs used for numerous mills on the river bank, this opened up the Fens to the river and canal system.

In 1831 a new channel was cut from Wisbech to the Wash, which brought further trade from the coast.

In 1845 the coming of the railways and improvement of roads led to a decrease in river use for trade and there was very little building and modernisation for the rest of the century.

In the 1930's many of the locks were updated and an electric lock was installed at the 'Dog in a Doublet', which was used to control the high water tides, which occasionally flooded up river as far as Peterborough.

Anti-flood measures were also built for Northampton in the 1970's, when the washland scheme and Bedford Road sluice gates were constructed.

Nowadays, the river and its environs are mainly used for pleasure, sport and recreation.

Linda Kemp 2008

RIVERS OF NORTHAMPTONSHIRE

Apart from the river Nene, four other rivers also rise in Northamptonshire.

They are:-

Leam - which rises near Arbury Hill.

Avon and Welland – which both rise near Naseby.

Ouse – which rises north of Brackley.

All rivers flow out of the county, none flow inwards.

Linda Kemp 2008

NORTHAMPTONSHIRE CANALS

The first canal in the county was the Oxford Canal in the west of the county which opened in 1778 and ran from near Coventry via Braunston to Banbury.

The main canal through the county was the Grand Junction which was authorised in 1793 and ran from the Oxford Canal at Braunston, via the Braunston and Blisworth tunnels, to Wolverton through Hertfordshire to the Thames at Brentford, a length of 93 miles and was completed in 1800 with the exception of the Blisworth tunnel. The first attempts at building the tunnel failed so until the tunnel was finally completed in 1805, a horse drawn tramway took boats over the hill between Blisworth and Stoke Bruerne.

BLISWORTH - TUNNEL -
STOKE - BRUERNE - ENTRANCE

In the north of the county the Leicester and Northamptonshire Union Canal was proposed to link the River Nene through Leicestershire to the Trent in

Nottingham. The southern part was started at Leicester, but was only partially completed to near Market Harborough by 1797, but in 1810 the idea was resurrected and by 1814 the Leicester and Grand Junction were joined at Buckby Wharf.

The route of the Grand Junction has been decided by the geography of the county as can be seen by the fact that the railway and later the M1 motorway follow roughly the same route, which meant that Northampton was not on the main canal route, but was joined to the canal at Blisworth in 1805 by a horse drawn tramway and finally in 1815 by the Northampton arm that joins the river Nene near Southbridge and as the Nene had been made navigable in 1761, this was the first time that the fenland waterways were connected to the main canal systems. From 1929 the Grand Junction Canal's name was changes to the Grand Union Canal.

The canals were important for the carriage of coal for heating and industry, goods, raw materials and food for the towns along the canal. They were also used for defence as at the Royal Ordnance Depot at Weedon Bec which started in 1804 and where the King and Cabinet would be brought to for safety in the case of a Napoleonic invasion.

Many of the villages and towns along the canals still have the remains of buildings which show the history, trade and living conditions of the people who worked and lived on the canals, especially the Canal Museum at Stoke Bruerne, Braunston, Blisworth, Cosworth, Buckby Wharf and Foxton just over the border in Leicestershire.

Top Lock and Museum (building on left)- Stoke Bruerne

Linda Kemp 2008

Passing Note – Fyn, Denmark.

On the part of Denmark called Fyn they still teach the children about how they traded with Northampton, prior to 1066, sailing up the Nene to Northampton to trade in timber, iron, leather, Welsh gold.

Question: Where would their birth place be, perhaps present day Bridge Street, or near the old town around near St. Peters or the Station? Or even Cow Meadow?

Tony Mallard 2007

WATERMILLS IN NORTHAMPTON

I have been a spinner and weaver for more than 30 years and always wondered about mills which would have been used to spin wool. There were several still working in Wales where I learnt to spin on a treadle wheel. 25 years ago, coming to live near Northampton, through which the Nene flows, this river must have been a vital source of power. Hence I started researching mills in the area, with the help of the Borough Council Community Programme, G.H Starmer and a fascinating lecture, given many years ago, by John H. Thornton.

History shows that the Romans brought the earliest mills to Britain, and the Saxons continued to build and use mills driven by water or animals to turn the wheels which ran the machinery. The Domesday Book mentions thousands of mills in Britain and many worked from the River Nene, such as Billing, Weston, Upton and Kingsthorpe, from the 11th. Century but were used to mill corn. Spinning of wool was a cottage industry at that time.

The source of the river Nene seems to rise from a lake north of Daventry and another from near Newnham south of Badby, and flows to Northampton, passing Upton and Duston Mills, where it joins the river in the town near the Cotton Mill. North from this famous old cotton mill, another source of the river comes from Maidwell near Kelmarsh, Naseby and between Guilsborough and Ravensthorpe. On this east side of Northampton, not far from the Cotton Mill, we find remnants of the Kingsthorpe South Mill. Originally it was leased to St. Andrews Priory and was let in 1529 as a corn mill to

Agnes Hayward, a widow, with Ambrose Walker and his wife Margaret. The value of the mill at this time was 49s 2d. In 1940 it was badly damaged by fire and demolished after World War Two. The site can be found from the end of Mill Lane in Semilong, across the road by Miller's Meadow.

Kingsthorpe Upper Mill

Further up river is Kingsthorpe Nether Mill, which was owned by Thomas Moss and known as 'Moss Mill'. It was demolished early in the 20th. Century and the area is now a nature reserve, as the route of the river is changed and flows under the road, Mill Lane, not too far down from the Cock Inn with paths and a lovely walk along the river, where signs of the mill race can be seen.

Up river again we come to Kingsthorpe North or 'Farre' Mill [as it was furthest away from the village]. It was leased in 1521 to John Hopkins and his wife Margaret. Until 1950 it was grinding corn into flour and then called 'Walkers Mill', and soon after it was vacated and became derelict.

One can see the mill-race by walking on a footpath from the housing estates near Leyland Drive (off Welford Road). This is a pleasant picnic place and can be reached by a similar path which continues down river to Kingsthorpe village.

Where the west and north tributaries meet south of Northampton, they converge at the site of the old Town or Cotton Mill. In 1742, due to the industrial revolution, the town mill (Kingsthorpe South) was converted to a power-driven mill and a steam engine installed by Edward Cave and worked by Richard Arkwright's skills and Hargreaves Spinning Jenny, which took over the textile production. Edward Cave, born and lived in nearby Rugby, heard that the water-driven corn mill in Northampton was for sale. He bought it, demolished it, and built what was to be the world's first power-driven mill. The cotton mill on the River Nene had 50 spindles for cotton spinning and 100 children and other hands were employed. Cave took on a supervisor called Thomas Yeoman who lived in St.Mary's Street, a manager, Mr. Harrison, a third person Mr. Payton, and a Mr. Redshaw possibly a foreman. The latter seems to have been staying in the Woolpack Inn, Northampton.

Mr. Cave spent much time in Northampton and was one of the founders of the Infirmary (now Northampton General Hospital) as his name appears on the list of subscribers after a meeting, on the 20th September 1743 of the "General & Very Great Meeting of the Nobility, Gentry & Clergy".

There is a sad entry in the Mercury of the admission to the hospital of a boy who had broken his arm and lost three of his fingers, which were torn off by one of the wheels in the mill.

The mill appeared to be on the decline in the late 1740's. Edward Cave died in 1754, William his son seems to have rented the mill to Lewis Paul, who had been interested in the mill before this, and he tried to keep it going but by 1756 it was advertised in the Mercury to be let or sold valued at a £1000. There was a final attempt to sell some machinery as late as 1765 and may have found its way to Lancashire.

Thomas Yeoman fled to France to avoid his creditors. However, that is not the end of the story, as the Mercury of 4th February 1792, fifty years after setting up the mill, carried another advertisement, announcing that Thomas Frost, a spinner, and J. Mico Gibson, described as a gentleman, gave notice that the spinning of cotton was dissolved and the business relinquished. In a later edition, Thomas Frost informs the public that in the consequence of the failure of the cotton trade, he has laid up a pair of French Stones and hopes to grind corn with the assistance of his steam engine.

After 60 years of cotton spinning the mill was back to grinding corn and run by the Perry family, then taken over by the Corporation in 1927 and pulled down in the 1930's.

Further east along the river there are many mills, Nunn Mill was given to the nuns at Delapre Abbey by the Queen in the 15th Century and was a corn mill later owned by the Bouverie family and leased to Joseph Westley from Blisworth. He used the river to transport wheat and coal from the boats. The site of this mill is now occupied by Avon Cosmetics. The river becomes very spread out and there are now water sports where Rushmills was situated. According to manuscripts in the

British Museum in the 13th. Century, it was known as "Rissemiln". Later in the 19th Century it made paper and even Postage stamps. Abington and Weston mills are also sites of ancient mills.

Further down river was Clifford Mill, then a short distance away there are remnants of Billing Mill, in the public house where the water-wheel can be seen, behind a glass screen. The mill race is rushing under the pub and there are other pieces of milling equipment around.

Billing Mill

The foreman, Tommy Mahony, was also from Limerick and Bartrums owned the business. They were making the flax into thread [very dusty work] to go to the spinning mills, towards the construction of parachutes. Out of their wages £4 per week, lodgings £1.5s. Mary and Maure (see recent photo below) were able to send home 10 shillings or even a £1, to help their families in Ireland. It is worth paying a visit to this Billing Mill Pub as it is the only representation of milling in the area.

Mary Barnes from Blasket Islands and Maure West from Limerick. Billing Mill W.W.2 staff.

Billing Mill

Apart from Billing, all the other mills were replaced by larger electrically powered mills and then newly established factories or just fell into disuse and only a few stones or rubble remain at the sites.

There is much water lying around the Aquadrome alongside Billing, the Nene now flows towards Cogenhoe and a very good sight of a mill race running under the building, once an old mill. The river makes its way to Wellingborough, through Wisbech, and on to the Wash, where it ends its journey to the sea.

Angela O'Dwyer 2007

WATER MILLS

Many mills in Saxon times were recorded in the Domesday Book, most villages having one and many had two or three.

Domesday records about 265 mills in Northamptonshire.

The Greek Mill (also known as Norse Mill or Northern Mill) was probably the earliest form of water mill.

GRIST MILL was for grinding corn, but specifically it was a small mill for grinding people's own corn. The corn they brought to the mill was called grist and sometimes the meal or flour they took away was called grist. Grist Mill could either be a water mill or a windmill.

CLACK MILL was always a corn mill. It got its name because of the clacking noise made by a clapper striking the hopper and causing the corn to be shaken on to the mill stones. The old water mill at VIGO, close to the windmill, was a Clack Mill

FULLING MILL (also known as a Cloth Mill or Woollen Mill) This was a mill in which cloth was fulled or milled, that is cleansed and thickened by washing and beating, it was cleansed with soap and/or Fullers Earth and beaten by wooden mallets which were let fall on it. Several Northamptonshire water mills were Fulling Mills, one of them being at ADSTONE.

CUTTLE MILL was a Fulling Mill that performed an operation on cloth. Cuttle means to fold cloth so as to lay it in cuttles or pleats. One was on the Watling Street in Paulerspury.

GYGG MILL. Gygg means something that whirls. A Gygg Mill was connected to a Fulling Mill and a Cuttle Mill. It raised the nap of the cloth. There was one of these mills on the Nene between Nunn Mills and South Bridge.

COTTON MILLS. The Town Mill (which was originally a corn mill owned by the town and known as Marvells Mill) on the Naseby branch of the Nene close by the gasworks, was converted to a cotton spinning mill in 1742. It was converted back to corn grinding in 1806.

PAPER MILLS. Some watermills in Northamptonshire have been paper mills, although doubtless all of them were converted corn mills. RUSH MILLS for instance commenced paper making in1833 and until 1888 government stamp paper and bank note paper was made there. Other examples of paper mills are VIGO PAPER MILL, WANSFORD PAPER MILL and GRAFTON REGIS PAPER MILL.

Mavis Cook 2006

COGENHOE MILL

There has been a mill at Cogenhoe since 1080 and possibly earlier than that. Cogenhoe Mill was a grist mill, producing mainly animal feed. The water power generated by the wheel was used for rolling oats and chaff cutting to make fodder for cattle and horses. There was also a blower for winnowing (removing the husks) and a set of rollers was used for cracking hemp seed for use by anglers as bait. Most water mills had an eel gleave to catch fish at the end of the day when the mill stopped working and Cogenhoe was one of these. It ceased to be a working mill in about 1950.

M.J.Cook 2007.

COGENHOE MILL (2)

Although the present building dates only from the 18th century, there has been a mill at Cogenhoe since at least the time of the Domesday Survey in the 1080s and possibly earlier than that. In the 20th century the mill was operated by the Walker family, Harry Walker being the last miller.

The sacks of corn, barley, or whatever arrived on horse-drawn carts or Harry collected them with his own, home-made lorry; a Ford Ten saloon, cut in half, making a cab, and a wooden, hand-built, lorry sided platform. The full sacks had to be closed by gathering the tops together and tied about six inches down. This was to enable them to be lifted by a chain hoist to the third floor of the mill. This chain hoist had a ring on the end of the chain which you fed the chain through, making a slip knot which you placed over the surplus sacking at the tie, and pulled tight. You then operated the hoist with a rope connected to a slipping pulley on the third floor. This rope could be operated on the ground floor or second floor, of course. On raising the sack the chain would tighten and take the sack up through trap doors in the floor to whichever floor it was needed. These traps had just a three-inch hole in the centre of the two doors and, as the sack was pulled through, they opened and fell back closed as the sack continued up. This hoist could only be used when the mill was working. (Because it was powered by the water wheel)

To start the mill wheel, which was in the mill race outside the milling room in its own shed, the sluice gate had to be raised, allowing the water to flow towards the wheel and, with a little bit of help, started to turn. The shaft was through the wall to the main drive, a wooden cogged wheel (wheel pit). About six feet in diameter, this changed the drive from horizontal motion to a vertical motion, driving the milling stones at the second floor level. Also this motion was used to drive the shafting on other floors using different sizes of pulleys to give differing speeds for other uses. The turning of the wooden cog drive would make quite a noise, creaking and groaning. Now the sacks taken up to the top floor could be stored or used as they arrived, emptied into a floor-level hopper to feed down to the grinding stones. To keep the corn moving the hopper was shaken by another contraption again taken from the (lay) shaft, by leather belting. The idea of having the grinding stones on the second floor was to allow the rough flour from the grinders to fall into sacks through wooden square pipes that had a wooden shut-off slider to stop the flour whilst changing the full sacks. Whist grinding, the empty sack would be held open by two hooks and the bottom of the sacks would rest on a two-foot high wooden removable table. This was to assist the lifting of full sacks by hand to be loaded on the cart or lorry for the delivery.

Taken from an article written by Norman Poole

Chapter 8
HOLY MATTERS

SAINT PETER'S CHURCH

I remember when I was very young, perhaps 7 or 8 my mother and I used to visit Aunt Peg and Uncle Ken in Byfield Road in St James, near the river. They both were involved with St. Peter's church; I think Ken was a sidesman or something. Aunt Peg, a couple of other women, and on occasions my mum and me would go along to the church and polish the pews, sweep and arrange the flowers on a Saturday afternoon for the service on Sunday. My job, which I loved, was to get out the cloths and the tin of Brasso and polish the big brass eagle lectern. I did this in stages as it would have taken ages to polish the whole thing in one go.

The eagle lectern is still there, but I noticed recently that it had been varnished. Now in my later years I see the wonderful carvings in this church with adult eyes, but they still fascinate me, more so now as I am able to appreciate their antiquity and the skill that was needed to carve them. Although St. Sep's is probably older and bigger I feel this church is a more beautiful and interesting structure.

Excavations nearby between 1980 and 1982 revealed Anglo-Saxon remains that indicated that there was a church in this area from a much earlier period, probably about 800. It seems probable that this St. Peter's was originally built by Simon de Senlis II, second Norman Earl of Northampton, sometime after 1110. The church's close proximity to the Castle and the large processional arch of a west door that can be seen over the west window indicate that this church may once have functioned as the chapel to the castle, the west door being large enough to admit a Royal procession for worship. This arch would have originally been recessed arch by arch, but was rebuilt flat over the west window, along with the rest of the tower in the late 17th century.

Inside standing before the vestry in the south aisle is a large Saxon stone slab reputed to be the reliquary lid of St. Ragener, nephew of St. Edmund of East Anglia and killed by the Danes in 870. It is believed that this stone was in the church as part of a shrine to St. Ragener until the Reformation when they threw it out. It was rediscovered built into the wall of a nearby brewery when it closed down. The carving is most interesting and fascinated me when I was a kid with its interlaced vines, animals and plants along with a human face – the face of G-D, the Foliate God, The Green Man!

Jack Plowman 2008

Holy Trinity/St. Pauls's Church

Holy Trinity/St Paul's Church Northampton

Holy Trinity Church is in the Diocese of Peterborough. It's parish stretches from the Cock Hotel, Kingsthorpe, along Kingsthorpe Grove covering most of Kingsthorpe Golf Club, Queens Park and Semilong ending at the boundary of Kings Heath.

Holy Trinity is a very large church possibly too large for the parish. It stands on a rise between Balfour and Edinburgh Roads. It was built from stone from a local quarry belonging to Lord and Lady Robinson. This quarry was located in the Kingsthorpe Grove area. The old vicarage in Kingsthorpe Grove and a remaining dry wall that runs along the left side of this road were also built from this stone. The church was consecrated in 1909.

My personal memories of this church and its hall are mostly from childhood. I was a Brownie there and can still remember dancing around the toadstool, endeavouring to pass another test that would result in a badge which I would proudly take home for my mother to sew onto my uniform. I still have a book named 'Flower Fairies' that I received from my Brown Owl. I can remember this old church room, which was full of splinters and dust which made you sneeze. I particularly remember the stage where my older sister let me fall from, resulting in my front teeth being knocked backwards. The panic of blood, fear of being toothless and what my mother would say caused us to rush down the jetty between the church and Stanhope Road, where I lived, for help. The result of this accident was a torturous brace being fitted that made me gag every time it was put into my mouth. In this hall most of the parish social events took place being jumble sales, mother's meetings, Brownies, Girl Guides, Boy Scouts and so many more. Sunday school also took place in this hall. We would receive a stamp with a picture of a scripture scene to stick into our Sunday school book each week. Sadly I didn't like Sunday school very much, I never did fill mine. I can still remember the shiny white paper that we were given to draw on with wax crayons.

Church Parade seemed to be every Sunday. The flag bearers would proudly walk down the aisle feeling important. Sermons seemed to go on forever. My friend and I would do silly things during this time, sometimes we would carefully untie the pigtail ribbons of the girl in front of us. We would then tie her ribbons to the back of her chair so when she stood up the chair would move with her.

We laughed at the lady's hats, most women wore hats then, and those trying to keep awake during the sermon, in fact, we giggled at everything, we always sat at the back. Easter Sunday we would go to church dressed in all our new Easter clothes, this was the day when we would wear white ankle socks instead of thick woollen knee socks declaring spring even if it was snowing. Easter was very special then. Every item we wore was new from sandals to hats. My mother would take my sisters and I to Leicester, to C & A or John Lewis for our new garb. It was one of the most longed for days of the year. We would set off from Derngate bus station with our sandwiches, so very excited.

Holy Trinity is very special to me, I was baptized and confirmed there, as are my children, I was married there and my parents' ashes are buried in the small garden in front of the church. Many of the local residents and neighbours have chosen this option, I feel very happy thinking that my parents are with those they liked and respected. I do occasionally attend a church service there, this usually is when my friend comes to stay with me from the States. Although the church service is much higher than it was when we were children, old neighbours and school friends recognise us and make us feel very welcome.

Pauline Etheridge 2008

UNITARIANS IN NORTHAMPTON

Unitarian Church Abington Square

It was in 1827 that a number of the congregation of Castle Hill Meeting chose to leave and start a church professing Unitarian principles.

Unitarians believe in one God and reject the idea of the Father, Son and Holy Ghost believing that Jesus was a great prophet inspired by the Almighty but not a direct incarnation of God.

They first met at the Fountain Inn which once stood on the corner of Bradshaw Street and Silver Street. This pub later changed its name to the Criterion and then still later, moved over the road when the area was cleared in 1938 to build the Fish Market. The pub is now called the Boston Clipper. They soon bought a former old chapel in King Street.

In 1843 the young Phillip Manfield, a Bristol Unitarian moved to Northampton and began his career in the boot and shoe industry. By the 1890s Sir [as he was then] Manfield and Lady Manfield provided the money to purchase a piece of land and build a new purpose-built church on the Kettering Road near Abington Square. This was called 'The Kettering Road Free Church'. And it was here in the 1960s that I first came across Unitarianism.

At the time I was working for Peace News, a paper devoted to the peace movement. I and a colleague were covering this part of the march from Land's End to Holy Loch [a protest against American Nuclear submarines being stationed here]. He was a Unitarian and dragged me along to a service one Sunday. I liked the idea as he said, 'that one could preach from Robinson Crusoe if you felt it was relevant' and the no-nonsense logical attitude of Unitarianism appealed to me. However, being then in my teens, a Beatnik and still discovering the world about me I didn't return until I got involved with the World Congress of Faiths in the 1980s, one of the committee being the local Unitarian Minister.

The old church could seat 400 and I can remember in the 1960s when I visited it, there was something like 30 or so at the service – a light sprinkling among the pews. When I returned 20 or so years later there were 6 of us and we met in a little room at the front of the church! I understand that when it was in its hey-day there would be two services every week. One in the morning for the more wealthy members for many of the 'big names' in trade and local government were Unitarians in this town and another in the afternoon for their servants who would have been preparing the Sunday lunch in the morning. Both services were always full it seems.

Around the year 2000 we sold the church and moved to new premises in Hazelwood Road. We now have between eight and fifteen people to our services. Like all churches we have, over the years seen a decline in numbers, but now we seem to be increasing perhaps because of our appeal to individuals who prefer to think for themselves rather than be told what to believe. We have a fine history of clever people, local and national, being Unitarians right up to the present day – the inventor of the World Wide Web is a Unitarian!

Jack Plowman 2008

ST. PAUL'S CHURCH

This story was told to me by my father, Walter Spittles, it concerns a brass band. My father played the cornet in the 'Northampton Imperial Brass Band'. The brass band in my story was before my time but my father told me that in his day, an age when most churches had a brass band, this was the case with St Paul's Church.

This story is of a tragedy and a lost tradition.

The church rooms had a fire in which all the band instruments were destroyed and it seemed to be unlikely they could be replaced. The publican of the 'Queen

Victoria Tavern' on the corner of Kingsthorpe Main Road and Semilong Road was not a religious man by any means, but as the town in those days was made of districts (who looked after themselves) he decided to pay for a new complete set of instruments for the church.

In recognition of such a fine offer the vicar decided that on Sunday mornings the band would form-up and play on the march from the 'Queen Vic,' up to the church as a show of gratitude.

Now comes the loss of tradition!!!

Time passed, the vicar was replaced and after a while the new vicar decided it was not a good thing that a holy brass band should start from a public house and so the tradition was lost.

Reg Spittles 2008

CHRIST CHURCH

I was born in 1918, although I enjoyed reading, I always had more satisfaction to listen to older people of previous years, which in time to come would only come from reading books, not always the truth, just someone's opinion.

This is a story told to me in my schooldays by my uncle, Albert Randall, he was a surveyor who worked with the architect Matthew Holding, who designed the church known as 'Christchurch'. It stands in a very prominent position at the junction of the Wellingborough Road and Christchurch Road.

In the days that it was built, Northampton was a small market town but slowly expanding. The custom was that local businessmen for whatever reason would sponsor something or other, this was the case with 'Christchurch', some of the money would come from sponsors.

My Uncle Albert came from Sheffield, he always referred to money as 'brass'. When they were about to start building, he thought they'd be a bit short of 'brass' and while they had it they should build the front first, unfortunately they didn't.

After a time it appeared a further round of donations would be required and unfortunately one of the sponsors rather than make a donation withdrew. That made certain the 'Christchurch' would not be completed.

Uncle Albert's idea was that if they started at the front and had then run out of 'brass, the rear could have been tidied up with a real chance at a later date to continue further building, but they would still have had a complete church.

Reg Spittles 2008

Chapter 9
COMINGS AND GOINGS

NORTHAMPTONSHIRE TRANSPORTEES.

Benjamin Eaton, Woodford to Western Australia.

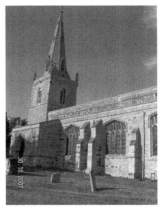

St Mary's Church dates from the 12th Century; it dominates from a high point overlooking green fields and the silver river below. There was a highly unpopular tax on baptisms and burials, levied by the government that led to the numbers of baptisms going down. Burials, however, could not be avoided. Its' parish registers show that the surname Eaton appears there from the 15th Century. It was noted by the Vicar in the late 1690s that there were un-baptised children of Francis, Thomas and Phillip Eaton who were given the label dissenters. Eaton burials do appear.

Sadly, as their beliefs were different, the whole Eaton line cannot be drawn. I believe that the parish records are incomplete too; I was told by some of the local people that one eccentric Vicar kept his goats in the Church who decided to eat at least one of these valuable books.

In 1815 John Eaton married Ann Swingler at Woodford and on the 13th April 1817 their first son, Benjamin, was christened, four other children followed but it is Benjamin who has gone down in history.

Schooling was not commonplace then. In 1819 there was an unendowed school with payments made by parents, there was a Sunday school where both adults and children may have been taught to read. There was also a Baptist run Sunday school. Work for all male children began from the age of 9 years or even earlier if the family was very poor.

The National school was not started until 1858, before this a Miss Arbuthnot set up a charity school, appearing in records in 1849.

On the 17th October 1839 at the church of Great Addington, Benjamin Eaton and Mary Ann Harris married, he was of full age but she was just 17 years old. His occupation is given as labourer and hers as a servant, he signed his name indicating that he had been taught, while Mary Ann made her mark. Benjamin's brother William was a witness to the marriage but he just made his mark.

The couple are found in the 1841 census living in Hog Lane, Woodford (now renamed Club Lane), he is an agricultural labourer and they have a 9 months old daughter, Louisa.

Pictured is where they lived.
The picture was kindly provided by Annette Del Bianco
From an original produced by Cyril Diamond of Thrapston

Life must have been fairly good for them at this time. General Charles Arbuthnot, who had joined the Grenadier Guards in 1816, lived at Woodford House and employed eleven servants. The late Elsie Dixon wrote that he employed Benjamin as a groom/coachman. She also states that General Arbuthnot moved to Warwickshire taking with him some of his servants, amongst them were the Eaton family. While they were living in Coleshill Mary Ann gave birth in 1849 to their fifth child. By 1850 they were back in Woodford as shown in the parish registers when their sixth child, Benjamin was baptised on the 3rd August and buried within a few days.

Our next certainty is that Benjamin Eaton appeared in court at Northampton charged with arson. An account of the trial appeared in the Northampton Mercury for the Lent Assizes in March 1851. On the Criminal side the business was excessively heavy, double that of the previous year.

Incendiarism at Woodford. After all the evidence was heard the jury, perhaps heeding the words of His Lordship who had said that it was desirable that bills should not be found on insufficient evidence, could not agree, after a long deliberation on a verdict.

They were allowed to retire. A fresh jury was empanelled, and several prisoners were arraigned. At length the jury came into Court with a verdict of guilty.

The Northampton Herald, Saturday, March 8 1851 carried the following article.

Arson at Woodford. Benjamin Eaton (34) for setting fire to a stack of straw, belonging to Joseph Walker. Prosecutor is a farmer of Woodford. On the 13th of

January last, about half-past 5 o'clock, heard a cry of 'fire'. Saw the fire out of his chamber window. It was in a stack of wheat straw. He dressed and went to it; when he got there the fire had been put out. The fire had been on the windy side of the stack, about a foot from the ground. John Mitchell is a surveyor of highways for Woodford. Early on the morning of 13th of January was called up by his servant, who said that there was a fire in his yard. He found a stack of barley straw in his yard on fire, and saw a stack belonging to Mr.Walker, just catching fire. Saw the prisoner in the village at the blacksmith's shop on the Thursday before the fire. Prisoner had been in his employ as one of the surveyors of the highways of Woodford. The wind blew from Mr.Walker's stack towards witnesses. Witness took possession of Mr.Walker's land at Michaelmas; at the time of the fire was in possession of the land on which Mr.Walker's stack stood.

Had complained to the prisoner for stopping away from his work too long at his meals. He said he would stay half-an-hour. Witness said he should make a deduction in his pay if he did. Prisoner was much put out at this. – John Millworth said the first cry of 'fire' he heard was at Mr.Mitchell's. As he was running there, on passing Mr.Walker's, he turned his head and observed fire burst out in Mr.Walker's yard. He went down the yard and saw a man standing at the end of the wheat hovel. The moment he perceived him, the man ran away. Ran after him but he could not tell who he was. Prisoner lived at the bottom of the lane. – A labourer, who lives in the lane between Mr.Walker's orchard and prisoner's house, deposed that as he was lighting his fire, on the morning of the fire, he heard someone run very fast past his house. Could not tell which way the person went, but the lane ascending steeply towards the orchard, he believed, from the rate at which the person ran, he must have been running from the orchard. – Mr.Evans, police-superintendent, went to the fire between eleven and twelve o'clock. The fire was out. Went into the orchard and found several footmarks straight down the orchard and into the lane towards the prisoners house.

Measured the marks. They were the marks of a man running; the strides were long; the runner appeared to have slipped; it was grassland, rather clayey. Measured several footmarks. One particularly plain mark in the orchard; about 20 yards from the fire, measured exactly 11½ inches. Went to prisoner's house. His shoes measured exactly 11½ inches. Took his shoes off and went into the orchard again. Made an impression by the side of the plain footmark. There were 18 nails in one boot, and in the impression alluded to there were the same number of marks of nails. The heels of the boots had a grooved plate round them. The footmarks contained impressions corresponding with the plate. Then apprehended the prisoner on charge of arson. Afterwards searched his house and found some naphtha, and a singeing iron. He had, he said, been singeing a horse. Witness produced the shoes and explained the peculiar marks in the shoes corresponding with the impressions. John Jeff's, police-inspector, found a portion of root in the prisoner's pocket which burnt strongly and acted as a slow match. Observed footmarks in the orchard in the direction of prisoner's house. – Prisoner's statement, on his committal, was, that he heard of the fire and went to it; as he was going, Joseph Wadsworth met him and told him that the rick yard was all on fire; saw some persons running away.- The Jury, after consulting a considerable time, retired, and a fresh jury was sworn. The jury, sometime afterwards, returned a verdict of guilty. – Fifteen years transportation.

Pictured here is the No.1.Court at Northampton that dates from c1678. In one corner of the beautiful ornamental plasterwork on the ceiling is a devils mask with a loosely fitting tongue, tradition has it that at the sound of false evidence the tongue is said to wag

In the 1851 census of March 30th we find Mary Ann with her children at Woodford: - Mary Ann Eaton   Head of house. Married 38 'Transports wife'   b Gt.Addington
Louisa Eaton   dau   10
b Woodford

William Eaton	son	9	
Shoemaker	"		
Samuel Eaton	son	7	Scholar
"			
Jane Eaton	dau	3	
"			
Mary Ann	dau	2	

b Warwicks, Coleshill

On the night of that census Benjamin was listed as being held in the Northampton Gaol.

August 1851 their seventh child is baptised, at Woodford, another Benjamin.

We can only imagine how the family survived the years to come; there are no records to show how they managed to live. Young William is at work and maybe Samuel would soon follow.

The workhouse had by then, replaced parish relief. These places had such a bad reputation that only in the most dire of circumstances would you enter. There was a Thrapston Union Workhouse that covered 26 parishes in all but no records survive before 1901.

The parish records for St. Mary's' show that the young Benjamin was buried on 15th April 1855. He was three and a half and died from 'fever and pneumonia'. This could indicate that the family had managed to stay in the village.

To take up the story for Benjamin, the convict. He was taken from Northampton and detained on a hulk.

Poverty in England led to a great upsurge in crime, many of the offences were food related with either food being stolen or something else that could easily be sold to pay for food. Many of these crimes would be seen as petty today, but then we are not starving. Before the

American war of Independence Britain had transported some 50,000 prisoners to those shores. When this practise stopped the prisons began to quickly fill.

A solution had to be found and thousands, awaiting transportation, were crowded onto decommissioned naval vessels or condemned ships called hulks. Conditions soon became as bad as in the prisons and then worse followed, hygiene was very poor and disease spread quickly. These 'temporary' measures set up by the government of the day were used over a period of eighty years.

The majority of the prisoners served the first two years of their sentence on a hulk. While on the hulks prisoners were put to good use, during daylight hours they were put to work either onboard painting or shipbuilding or ashore cleansing the rivers, but always in irons. For this work they received no payment during that time, a prisoner could be paid after the two years but never received the money, just benefits in food etc. Some proved such good workers they were kept back for several years.

This is the hulk pictured at Woolwich, London; this ship was destroyed by fire in 1857

Benjamin was given the number 1234 and detained on the hulk Defence.

On the 30th October 1852 he was transferred from Woolwich and on the 17th November left Plymouth heading for Western Australia, a new colony dating from 1829. In 1850 the first convicts were sent there as it is thought that the local settlers needed a supply of cheap labour to help develop the region. In all 9,720 convicts were sent until 1868 when the practise ceased.

The ship was the Dudbrook, a 601-ton barque built in Dundee in 1848. Its' destination was the Swan River Colony and carried 103 passengers and 228 convicts. As well as Benjamin, now prisoner 1619, there were two other Northamptonshire men. **Edward Bowe** from Daventry, a shoemaker sentenced in 1850 to 14 years for robbery with violence. He had assaulted a John Horn at Daventry and 'stolen from his person ten £5 notes, a sovereign and silver coins'. **James Hearn** was the other; he had been found guilty of 'uttering a forged bill of exchange' and was sentenced to serve 10 years. A convicted person who was sentenced to a term of 7 years or over was a candidate for transportation.

The shipboard description has: Eaton, occupation groom, married with 6 children. Height 5ft 4½ inches, of slight build, brown haired, hazel eyes, long faced and with a sallow complexion. Soon after sailing he was on the sick list for five days with diarrhoea. The voyage took 77 days arriving on the 7th February 1853 with no deaths recorded. His first sight of Australia would probably have been from Fremantle Prison.

On the 3rd June 1854 a ticket of leave was granted to Benjamin. This was to enable him the freedom to work and live within a given district. The convict could be self-employed or hire himself out. Conditions attached to this meant he had to attend church and to appear before the magistrates when required. It is thought that he worked as a groom. Around this time he made an application for his family to join him. He must have been thought of as a reliable working man and permission was granted.

Mary Ann and their five children are thought to have sailed on the Sir William Ffolks leaving England on the 2nd August 1855 and arriving in Australia 13th December that year.

In 1856 the family moved to Albany where Benjamin worked as a convict labourer. He was granted a conditional pardon on 1st January 1858.

January 1859 saw the birth of twins, Eliza and George, followed in 1861 by their last child, a daughter Annie.

Their daughter Jane was 17 years old when she was married in July 1862 to John Underwood Green.
Sadly just 6 months later Benjamin Eaton at the age of 46 years died from cancer.

In the Registry Office at Albany in 1866 Mary Ann married again, her husband was John Mattock, a widower, a sawyer by trade. Four years later she died, cause of death given as 'paralysis and disease of the brain'. It is known that she had been confined to a wheelchair and tended to by her daughter Jane.

Of their family: -
Louisa 1840-1861 married in 1860 Robert Williams, he was a Mounted Police Constable and the son of John

Williams who was a pensioner guard of the 51st Regiment.

William 1842-1919 married Emma Langoulant they had eight children.

Samuel 1843-96 married Mary Ann Rooney they had eight children

Jane 1846-1934 married John Green they had twelve children.

Mary Ann 1847-1907 married Joseph Brand they had five children.

George 1858-1932 remained single

Eliza 1858-1938 married 1) Peter Alston married 2) Thomas Reynolds and had eight children.

Annie, nothing is known.

Many of the descendants of Benjamin Eaton now live in the Perth area and I am indebted for most of this family information to a written account by his Gt.Grandaughter Elsie Dixon (now deceased). My thanks also go to his three times Gt.Grandaughter, Annette Del Bianco who has added to the story and allowed me to use it.

Thomas Jolly

A population count of 1831 recorded that there were 639 people living in Woodford, it is, I think, surprising to find that from this small number we have another transportee.

Thomas Jolly is found in the 1841 census working as a male servant in the employ of Mr .Palmer who is a farmer.

On the 4th March 1844 Thomas Jolly, aged 19 years, appeared in court at Northampton Assizes. He was accused of burglary stealing from Joseph Palmer a watch, butter and meat. He was found guilty and sentenced to a 10-year term. Jolly was not kept on a hulk and left his homeland on the Maria Somes on 22nd April 1844, arriving 96 days later at Van Diemen's Land (now Tasmania). Although he was in trouble again in 1846 he appears to have settled down and permission was given for him to marry an Irish convict Jane Connors in 1852.

Thomas Bland
About 4 miles away from Woodford is Thrapston and there we have Thomas Bland who was born circa 1819 the son of Thomas a stonemason.

Thomas junior married Ann Wallis who was eight years older than him and they had 5 children by the time Thomas got into serious trouble.

The Northampton Mercury reported that the case was heard on 5th March 1850: -

At Aldwinckle William Wills was employed as a watcher by Lord Lilford when on January 20th 1850 he, and a companion Samuel Carpenter, had seen a man sitting on a stile and four more beating a field for game. On approaching the offenders 'I said " You've been a beating for game my lads". Bland answered, "it's a d----d lie" and struck me immediately. Wills caught Bland by the collar and then the others all joined in the fighting. When Wills let go of Bland all the offenders made off, however Wills had been cut on the hand and he knew Bland and said that he was the one that had cut him, he also had a head injury.

The outcome of the trial was that Bland was a guilty man; the Learned Judge said that there had been a previous conviction for felony and that this was a brutal and violent attack on those who were lawfully protecting the property of an employer. He was sentenced to ten years transportation.

Bland was a carpenter and must have proved a very useful worker, as he never left England until December 1853. He was granted his ticket of leave before he arrived in Western Australia in May 1854.

There is no record shown of a family application being made and in fact they seem to have done fairly well without him, with the exception of 1851 where his wife Ann 41 years old is listed as a pauper (incidentally she was born at Woodford).

In that census we also have with her, John 11 - Sarah Ann 9 - William 6 - James 5 and Samuel 2 years. Ten years later Ann at 51 years is a laundress; in 1871 she is listed as Ann Pain, a widow. A few years after an enforced transportation separation marriage to a new spouse was allowed.

John became a Blacksmith, married Mary Ann Pain and had 7 children.

Sarah Ann married in 1862 (and said her father was Thomas Bland, labourer) Thomas Oliver.

William became an Ironstone labourer and lived at Woodford with his wife Abigail Hawes who was born there. They had 8 children. It is probably just coincidence as I have found no proof of relationship but Abigail was the daughter of John Hawes and a Sarah Eaton.

James became a milk purveyor; he married Emma Lowe and had 5 children.

Samuel was a builder's labourer and moved to Hornsey, Middx. His first wife was Susan. His second wife was Eliza; they had at least 4 children.

J.M. Clements

YARDLEY HASTING TO VAN DIEMEN'S LAND

A trial took place at Northampton on March 4th 1841 of three men from the nearby village of Yardley Hastings. The case promoted much local interest and the courtroom was full to suffocation point as reported in the Northampton Mercury of 6th March.

The men stood accused of causing the death of John Dunkley, who was a watcher of game working under the head gamekeeper, Mr.Longstaffe, both in the employ of the Marquis of Northampton.

The three accused were James Underwood, 21 a farm worker. Joseph Bedford also 21, a farm worker, and William Downing, 31.

On the evening of Tuesday 6th October 1841 John Dunkley did not return home, nor did he on the following night. This obviously caused his wife much concern and she went to Mr. Longstaffe to inform him of this. A search party was set up on the 8th and this was when the unfortunate man was found dead, his head covered in blood, nearby they had found traces of blood and part of a gunstock.

Mr. Adams opened for the prosecution by calling several witnesses, Joseph Longland stated that he had seen the prisoners drinking in a pub at 2.30pm on the 6th and that Underwood had asked him many times to lend him a gun. On being refused this he pressed to buy one, he was 'very serious to get a gun', saying he must have one for that night as they were going on a spree.

Later Downing had left the pub; he probably went home to fetch his gun. He was seen by Joseph Longland (a boy) to drop a gun barrel from his pocket when he climbed over some poles.

George Whitely, a labourer, saw Bedford at about 6pm and warned him that he had seen a keeper going the way that he was going. He saw the others join him. At about 6.30 the witness heard 2 reports of guns close together, somebody screamed and another gunshot was heard.

Mr. John Pell, surgeon, gave evidence that on the Friday he subjected the body to a strict examination and found cuts to the eye-lid and upper lid, a wound to the top of the head, and another that had severed the right ear from the head. There was also a gunshot wound to the neck. The charge had passed through the deceased's collar and been dispersed about the scapulary muscle. There was also a 4 inch lacerated wound on the back of the head connected with an irregular fracture of the skull penetrating to the brain. A violent blow from a gun or any other blunt instrument might produce such a wound.

Suspicion fell on the prisoners; they were found working near the Rose & Crown Pub at Mr.Riddles' premises and taken to Castle Ashby. Their homes and living quarters were searched. At Bedford's lodgings a pair of cord breaches were found that were quite wet in places, with marks of blood recently washed out. At Downings' lodgings a jacket with spots of blood on the left arm and shoulder was found. After searching Underwood's (where nothing was found) Bedford was brought into the custody of a constable. Bedford was examined and found to have about 30 gunshots in his back and arms; he said that John Dunkley was responsible.

Bedford's own version of the whole story was given. It emerged that he and Underwood had been working together when the threshing machine broke down; as they had nothing better to do they decided to go to the pub. After eating their victuals and downing a gallon of beer, Phoebe Bedford had thoughtfully taken her sons dinner to the pub, the machine mender came to the pub and said the repair couldn't be done that day, as parts had to go to the blacksmith's. Bedford then helped taking some parts to the Blacksmiths' shop. He and Underwood went to the Rose and Crown, this is where they met up with Downing and they all drank there until around 5.30pm. Downing left them to go to his home and they all met up again making for an area called New Hay.

Bedford said that he saw a hare and took a shot at it but missed. The sound of the shot alerted John Dunkley and he was seen to approach, Underwood and Downing went one way while Bedford another, however the way he chose brought him face to face with the watcher. We had a word with each other, and some way or another he cocked his gun and I did mine, and whether his went off first or mine I can't tell, but I think mine did. His shot caught me in the left shoulder and I fell upon the gun I had in my hand. I was on the ground when Dunkley passed me, and he swore at me dreadful. This was when Underwood and Downing joined him, and on seeing that Bedford had been shot they started after Dunkley. The statement continued...they went down to the Riding and shot him, I went after them. Jim had a hold on Dunkley who said you mean to stand this do you Billy and pushed his gun at Bill. I had hold of Dunkley's gun muzzle. Bill stepped backwards and cocked his gun and shot Dunkley who fell. I had hold of his gun when he fell and I struck it as hard onto the ground, as hard as ever I could and the stock broke in two. I threw the gun down and Jim kicked him and hit him with the gun. Then Downing at his legs and Jim at his hands they dragged him about 16 yards off the path. The three went off to the village of Olney, hiding a gun in a hedge there and then went for a drink in the pub.

Mr. Miller, who was for the defence, and said that the prisoners had gone out on that day without intent to harm or kill. He must have argued the case well, even saying that the prisoners had been afraid for their own lives. The prisoners were found guilty, not of murder, but of 'very aggravated manslaughter'. Transportation for life was the sentence.

The parish records for the burial of John Dunkley (39 years old) on the 11th October have a note written by the vicar that states 'this poor man was murdered by Joseph Bedford, William Downing and James Underwood who are already this moment confined in Northampton gaol'. A later note was added after the trial saying the three were to be transported for life.

The three men were transferred from Northampton to the hulk 'Laviathan' in Portsmouth. From here Bedford wrote several notes to his parents and to his sister Emma. Two 'coins' were hammered out, one to another sister, Martha, and one to his mother that says

Mother the year rolls round and steals away the breath that first gave it whateer we do whateer we be, weer travelling to the grave though men despise me and revile I count the trial small whoever frowns if Jesus smiles it makes amends for all Your unfortunate son J. Bedford transported for life 1841.

Their ship was HMS Tortoise, a Naval ship of 1,000 tons, it sailed from Plymouth on the 26th October 1842. The journey to Van Diemen's Land (re-named Tasmania in 1853) lasted 116 days without stopping. They arrived in Hobart Town on the 19th February 1843. This was the only time this ship was used as convict transport.

William Downing, was the only married man. He had left behind his wife, Hannah aged 26 and a two year old son, William. He also hammered out a coin that said

The judge meant to dispence for injurd innocence. Dear wife and boy hope without me you will have more comfort an joy. WD HD. False witnesses did rise up they laid to my charge things that I do not in my defence incage and their insulting rage.

He was 32 years old when he arrived and was in trouble at least twice before getting his ticket of leave in 1850, in this same year he married Sarah Brooks. His conditional pardon was granted in 1853.

James Underwood was quite settled into his sentence, he was only in trouble once for a fairly minor offence. He was working in Launceston in 1848. His ticket of leave was granted in April 1850 and a conditional pardon granted in 1854. He applied to marry Bridget Keleher (Kelly?) in 1852 and according to records Catherine Maguire in 1853.

He and Catherine were married on the 14th March
1853 in Hobart, he was 30 and she 22. Catherine, alias
Ann Melia, alias Ellen Murray had arrived in V.D.L. on
the Aurora two years previously. Her transportation (7
years) was for larceny and a previous conviction of
felony, her description was 5ft 1 inch, sallow complexion
and red hair. Her native place was given as Liverpool
where she had lived with her husband William Melia for
12 months they had a child.

James and Catherine had nine children: -

James 1854-1940 married Jane Williams m2 Florence
Smith

Thomas 1855-1951 married Elizabeth Williams = 5
children

Joseph 1858-1923 married Elizabeth Ralph = 6 children

Ellen 1860-1949 married James Hicks.

John 1862-1922

Jesse 1864-1935 married 1) Mary Dimpson =3 children

m2) Annie Russell= 3 children

m3) Lila Cripps.

Sarah 1866-   married 1887 Stephen Wright = 1 child

m2) James Scoles.

Son b 1868   and a daughter Mary born 1871.

Catherine Underwood died in March 1912 aged 82 years.
Seven carriages followed the coffin.

James Underwood died at the great age of 94 years in
June 1913, six carriages followed on.

Joseph Bedford, at 22 when he arrived, his behaviour
was good to start but then he became a rebel around
1844. In June of that year he was found with tobacco in

his possession, for this his probationary period of three years was extended.

On March 13th 1845 he was sentenced to 12 months hard labour in chains in the coal mines for insubordination, he had broken out of his hut at night. On the 5th April he was absent from the mines without leave and 36 lashes were given as punishment. Two days later he was again in trouble for taking off his irons.

In another attempt to escape he had been caught with other prisoners trying to build a boat.

He was eventually released from the mines in June 1846. It was agreed by the Lieutenant Governor that Bedford should be sent to Port Arthur from the coalmines to be with the 'old class of convicts'. At some point he managed to get himself 7 days in solitary confinement as punishment for being found in the bedroom of his masters female servant.

He was accused, on several occasions, by a Henry Keach of sheep stealing but was lucky enough to be found not guilty each time.

Despite all of this his conditional pardon was approved in June 1853. He applied for permission and married Sarah Briggs (who was the daughter of a free settler from Yorkshire) and they produced seven children. (Even then he had 'dallied' with another woman and produced an illegitimate son).

Six of their children survived, his daughter Elizabeth died when she was 15 years old. All but one of his remaining children moved to New South Wales. Sarah died in 1903 and Joseph moved in with his daughter Phoebe (named after his mother) and her family in Sydney. He died there in 1906 and is buried in the Field of Mars Cemetery.

I appreciate the help given me for information on the Bedford family given to me by Darren Emmett and Andrea Marks who are both direct descendants. Also much additional information came from Bob Taylor of Kent who is descended from William Bedford, older brother of Joseph and who, ironically, is shown as an under gamekeeper in the 1851 census. These people gave their blessings to any publication.

There were in the region of 1,000 convicts sent from Northamptonshire to Australia.

J.M.Clements 2007

FROM HANTS TO NORTHANTS.

Frederick Withers was born in Hampshire in 1841 and by the age of 20 years was already heading north. He is found in the 1861 census in Newbury as a grocers' assistant and by the 1871 census he was an established Groser with his own premises.

52, KETTERING ROAD.

A trade magazine of the times described it as 'one of the smartest business houses to be found in the suburbs of Northampton'. It also said that the business was conducted on strictly ready-money lines, this being absolutely necessary owing to the reasonable prices. A discount of half a penny in the shilling is however allowed, Mr.Withers being the first tradesman in the town to adopt this plan. A complete list of goods would be impossible to list in the article but Lazenby's and Batty's jams, sauces, pickles, preserved meat and fish were mentioned along with Huntley & Palmer's and Peek Frean's biscuits, sugars, rice, flour and spices were all to be found. All kinds of tea was also to be had ranging in price from 10d to 2 shillings a pound, these, it was boasted, came from growth in India, China and Ceylon. As well as grocery products brushes of all kinds, and various household requisites can be bought. The business had a connection with a branch shop at 92 & 94 Overstone Road, and a large patronage is naturally accorded them. The same advertisement says that the business is not confined to Northampton alone, for by aid of specially constructed vans, a wide district for many miles around is served.

Pictured are two of the earlier models of transport for the country rounds.

The motorised version, that came later.

Frederick F.Withers   c. 1863

Frederick had married a Northampton girl in 1864; she was Mary Ann Gross who was the daughter of a greengrocer who lived in Derngate. They had a total of 11 children but the last 4 did not survive infancy. Frederick died in 1891 at the age of 50. Of the seven children 4 were daughters who all married and produced children. It was a different story for the sons, the oldest was Frederick who married twice but never had any children, and he ran the shop in Overstone Road and later took premises in Kettering Road until his sudden death in 1919. George took over his fathers' enterprise but his heart was not in it and he was far more interested in breeding Sealyham dogs of which he had several show prizewinners. He had two children, a daughter and a son who carried on the business until just after World War 2.

Of the third son, he married in 1893 but had no children; he died in 1905 at the very early age of 33 years.

There are many descendants still in Northamptonshire.

Article written by his Gt.Grandaughter J.M.Clements in 2007

IT'S A LONG WAY TO TIPERARY

This is the story of my grandmother, Bridget Kelly, who arrived in England from her native Ireland and worked as a servant in Birkenhead as is shown in the 1901 English census. She was 19 years of age at that time.

At some point she became a domestic servant at the Grand Hotel here in Northampton, but her living accommodation was at Shipmans. It was here that she met her

future husband Charles Hodson who was a gardener, they married early in 1906 her address is given as 12 The Drapery.

This is their wedding photo; you can see that her left glove has been removed to show off her wedding ring.

They started their life together in Kingsthorpe, she was still in service for a while but then by the end of the year she had given birth to their first daughter. They rented a small house just ' 2 up and 2 down' opposite Kingsthorpe Recreation ground and five more daughters followed at regular intervals. During the 1914-18 war Charles worked as a gas fitter, because of his family commitments he was not called to go to war, but family legend has it that he received harsh words from workmates, joined up and served in the Northamptonshire Regiment. My mother told me she remembered him coming home on leave, entering through the front door and going straight through to the back garden where he would light a candle and burn the lice from his uniform seams. He was killed in action on the 4th April 1918. On the 14th May his last child, the son they had wanted was born.

My grandmother was left with 7 children to bring up on her own and 7 shillings and 6 pence per week to live on. She did have a hard life but she was fiercely proud of her family. She died in 1952 only ever having been back once to her homeland.

J.M.Clements   2006

WOMEN (mainly) WHO CAME AND SERVED ....

Many stayed and became the great grandparents etc of today's Northamptonians, as did Bridget Kelly, whose story is told by J. M. Clements.

Looking at census returns, late Victorian years, for quite another reason, I noted that many women had come to Northampton from far and wide to work in hotels and private houses as servants. The question then is why Northampton?

They could have left their homes because of lack of local employment, sometimes they followed their sisters or cousins, and some must have had a sense of adventure. Gentry wanted servants from 'away' so that they wouldn't gossip about the 'big house' to their families. Many would have answered an advertisement in a local paper of a publication such as Hotel and Tavern Advertiser or The Servants Register. Northampton had several Registry Offices for Servants based in town such as:-

Misses Betts   5 The Parade
   Misses Elliott   64 Marefair
   Mrs Henry Law   36a Gold Street
   Mrs H Millard   Corn Exchange

Girls were sometimes housed in dormitories until a position was found for them – not always quite the 'work' they expected.

Rail links of the time were good, eight trains a day in 1890 from London, the 7.15 a.m. arrived Northampton 9.14 a.m. People also came by river and canal. On census night in 1871, 9 boats were berthed, the crews came from such places as Lincoln, Loughborough, Stafford, Wolverhampton, Birmingham. The vessels had names such as The Mersey, The Victoria, The Albert, John Barrington. So from Midland Station St. John's Street or from South Bridge these weary but hopeful arrivals had their first glimpse of Northampton as they made their way up Bridge Street to their new employers.

Angel Hotel 1890   *Angel Hotel 2008*

Had they travelled by coach, the horse drawn variety, the road links would have been:-

Kingsthorpe Road from Leicester via Market Harborough,
Towcester Road from as far away as Holyhead via Watling Street,
Bedford Road coming from the Great North Road

Coach Times

Poster  *Heading*

and not forgetting the humble carrier's cart, which picked up in the outlying villages and plied trade in the town to and from inns in the area. Not the most comfortable way to travel, especially in winter, when if the driver was of good heart, a hot brick would be wrapped in sacking and placed at the feet of the passengers.

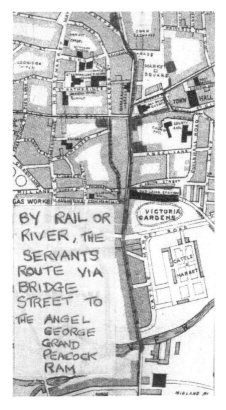

Hotels and Inns in the town were amongst employers of workers from outside the county. The Angel, The George, The Peacock had resident domestic staff and barmaids from far and wide in the late 1800s, such diverse places as Malta, Germany and Mayo, and from

Scotland to Kent. They must have been women of strength and courage to have left their families and to have journeyed to Northampton to work. Other places with resident staff were The Plough, The Ram and The Grand, to name but a few – sadly they are no more – The Grand is there in name only. The Peacock, a fine hotel was demolished in 1959. The George had suffered the same fate in 1921 to be rebuilt as a bank. The Angel – well the building is still there, but hard to imagine it was once a fine major coaching inn, a bustling place where many began their working lives in this town.

Map of Hotels

Off Angel Street is Fetter Street with what must be the last remaining cobbles in the town, not hard to imagine the horses' hooves slipping in wintry conditions.

Fetter Street cobbles

In the year 1881 Lewis George Moore was the licensed victualler of The George Hotel, by 1891 Sarah Henrietta Moore, his wife, was listed, but Lewis was found to be aboard "Merrie Duchess" at Sheppey with a crew of three. Had he become a man of means sailing for pleasure or was he pursuing a second career? The census returns give insights into people's lives, makes us ask questions, but unfortunately does not answer them all.

George Hotel Census

Another 'career' in hotels was that of Billiard Marker, usually quite a young man who kept scores and took bets, not a respected 'profession', but one that added colour to the establishment. George W. Basley aged 23 from Birmingham, Frederick H. Noale, 24, from Staffordshire and Herbert Nicholls, 22, from Worcestershire were just a few who were employed as such in local hotels.

Employed as a barmaid at The Angel in Bridge Street was Emma Major. It was reported in the Northampton Guardian that she was charged with attempted

---

...ngborough...
were fined 7s. each, or 7 days.

THE ATTEMPTED SUICIDE BY A BARMAID.

Emma Major, barmaid at the Angel Hotel, Bridge-street, was charged, on remand, with attempting to commit suicide by cutting her throat with a knife while in the Angel Hotel, on the 11th of August. The court and its precincts were crowded, and much sympathy seemed to be felt for the unfortunate position in which the young woman had placed herself.—Mr. Rawlins, junr., of Market Harborough, appeared on behalf of the accused.— The evidence given on Saturday by Miss Elizabeth Ann Dawkins, barmaid at the Angel Hotel, was again read over.—By Mr. Rawlins: She said she had had some disagreeable words with a gentleman. Did you gather who the gentleman was?—She gave me his name.—Mr. Rawlins: Be good enough to tell us.—It was Mr. Douthwaite.—Mr. Rawlins: Her conduct and manner on that occasion, I presume, were very different from what they had ordinarily been.—I had only known her a day.—Mr. Rawlins: Were you present at all at the interview between Douthwaite and her?—No; I know nothing of what took place between them but what she told me. —Mr. Rawlins: There was not much injury done? —No; very little.—Mrs. Amelia Holmes, wife of Mr. Henry Nicholas Holmes, of the Angel Hotel, said she heard Douthwaite call Miss Major some very unpleasant names in the coffee-room, about half-past ten o'clock on the previous night. Witness was asked to go into the room by Mr. Holmes, who said Miss Major and Douthwaite were quarrelling. Witness went into the coffee-room, but was not there at the commencement of the quarrel. They were having words when she went in; but she did not know what they were. Douthwaite afterwards 'd to witness, "You think you have a respectable

---

186

suicide 10th August 1882. Subsequently after 4 or 5 days in prison on sureties of £20 each, Emma was released into the care of her brother Arthur William Major a nurseryman from Oundle and her uncle William Major a clicker from Tanner Street. £20 must have been a lot of money for a clicker to raise. Central to the case was Frederick John Douthwaite of Lyveden Terrace, a police clerk, formerly an accountant from Stourbridge in Worcestershire. He was charged with threatening to murder Emma. This charge was withdrawn but it was stated that she had suffered oppression at the hands of this man for years.

Emma was born in Oundle, daughter of James and Martha. James was also a nurseryman/florist. After leaving The Angel Hotel, Emma worked as a housekeeper for a baker, a widower, and his family at Huxlor Place, Kettering.

Also working as a barmaid at the same time as Emma was Ellen (Nellie) Major, who was born in St. George in the East, London, in 1855, daughter of George and Anne. Nellie had worked as a servant in London prior to making the move to Northampton where her relative was.

This sad case highlights the often unhappy lot some women of the time encountered, sometimes trapped in work where they were at the mercy of unwanted attentions of senior staff or their employers. If the servant then became pregnant it was she who was dismissed, often to end up in the workhouse.

Harriet Crane was on 19th July 1893 charged with sleeping in an outhouse at Upper Heyford, without visible means of subsistence, she had no home. She was sentenced to 1 month's hard labour. Poor girl!

In 1882 Mary Smith, aged 22, was employed as a servant by Walter Alford Taylor, draper of 11 Abington Street. Mary was charged and found guilty of concealment of a birth, having hidden the baby under coal in the cellar. She was taken to the workhouse where she had been confined 2 years previously, later sentenced to 12 months hard labour. Was she bad or just desperate?

November 1882 Annie Reeve a knot tier aged only 11 of Quart Pot Lane, was found guilty of theft and was sentenced to 11 days imprisonment and 4 years in a reformatory. It was her 2nd offence and her father couldn't cope with her. A hard start to a young life.

Just three cases highlighting harshness and intolerance of those times.

Servants employed in private houses in the town were mostly, but not all, local women and contrary to popular belief not many were under 16 years of age.

Dr Rae's House in Abington Street

Dr.William Moxon resided in Derngate and Dr.William Rae in Abington St.

Both employed a page aged 13 and 14 in 1881 and 1891. (In the 1890s pages aged 10-16 years old were employed with a wage of £8-£16 per annum, depending on age, height, appearance and abilities – described as a boy servant, apprentice, footman or messenger, in large manor houses usually.) Both these respected men also had servants and cooks from outside the county. Dr George Percival also of Abington Street was the surgeon to the workhouse – were the three local women employed by him recruited from there?

Adelaide and Leicester Terraces were typical of private houses all over Northampton, listed in 1841 as having local occupants. The nearby Catholic Bishop's House had three staff recorded as not local, and the Priest Alphonse Awanger from 'foreign parts', the later Cathedral House had a very cosmopolitan list of residents over the years – from America, Brittany, Belgium and many from Ireland.

The terraces were four stories high, so for one sole servant it would have been a hard life carrying coal and water up the many stairs with the range below stairs. The cold attic was where she would have slept. A very lonely life for the girl with only one half day off a week if she was lucky. The heads of these houses were either connected to the church or shoe trade, employers or retired manufacturers. Unusual for a woman of the time, in 1851 Mary Eyston living at Leicester Terrace was listed as a mortgage proprietor. By 1871 William Barton, shoe manufacturer, was at 2 Adelaide Terrace. His wife's occupation was forewoman in shoe factory.

Was William out and about, leaving his wife to oversee the work?

Moving round to Hester Street, most of the houses seem to have lone live-in servants over the decades from 1871-1901 and yet again local women. But at number 8 in 1871 lived Hans Lursen, a leather merchant from Copenhagen. His wife originated from Liverpool. Did he sail to that city and not Newcastle or London? His two servants came from Lincolnshire and Warwickshire, the latter, the nurse, probably took her three charges to the Racecourse for an airing.

Some households were really not in a position to employ any staff, but had ideas above their station and would employ a young local girl at a pittance, sometimes it was only her keep, and some employed girls from the workhouse. These unfortunates were glad to have been given the chance to escape the confines of the institution, but often swapped one life of drudgery for another. Not having had a home life, never having been used to handling personal possessions or breakables, not ever been witness to the finer things in life, they fell short of their employers' expectations and incurred their wrath. Often they were dismissed to become destitute yet again, or kept trapped in a treadmill of menial chores, having to blacklead the grates and scrub floors long before breakfast was prepared. Sore knees, bad backs, reddened raw hands, not a job to be able to carry on with until old age!

Another employer of large groups of women from outside the county were shops such as Adnitts in The Drapery. The opposite side of the street was for a time known as The Glovery. One such store had in 1891 a resident staff of sixty, fifteen of them young men and the remainder women, mostly in their twenties working as shopwomen and dressmakers. They worked long hours, but it was still servitude, even so, preferable to a servant's life, at least they had the company of others their own age.

What about those who were unable to work ...... well it was the workhouse for them. NORTHAMPTON UNION WORKHOUSE, it was on the Wellingborough Road, opposite the then St Edmund's Church. Even the name brought a chill to many a poor soul in Northampton. It was opened in 1835 and remained as a workhouse until the 1930s.

The figures for census returns show a higher number of women inmates than men, it seemed they lived longer. Most female former occupations were shown as domestic servant or charwoman (the daily women) or laundress, with the occasional lace maker or dressmaker. There were nearly as many from far flung places as from Northampton. Amongst the inmates were whole families, the children separated from the adults, the wives separated from their husbands. There were siblings and there were orphans. If a servant from miles away became too ill or too old to work, she wouldn't have had the means to travel back to her home so the only option was ..... The Workhouse.

THE WORKHOUSE.

Liberal provision was made at the Northampton Union Workhouse to impart the joys of Christmastide to the inmates, whose wants had received the considerate attention of many ladies and gentlemen of the town. At half-past seven in the morning breakfast, consisting of coffee and bread and butter for all, was served; and during the forenoon the men were supplied with tobacco, the women with snuff, and the children with oranges. The dinner, as usual, was provided at noon, and it consisted of roast beef, baked potatoes, and boiled plum pudding, half a pint of beer being also allowed to each inmate. It may be interesting to say that the quantities were as follows:—449lbs. of beef, 450lbs. of potatoes, and the ingredients of the pudding, 60lbs. of currants, 60lbs. of raisins, 7lbs. of peel, 40lbs. of sugar, ¾lb. of ginger, 1lb. of spice, 2lbs. of baking powder, 78 eggs, and 24 quarts of milk. The following visitors were present during the meal, and zealously attended to the wants of the inmates: The Mayor and Mayoress (Alderman H. E. and Mrs. Randall, who were specially welcomed by members of the Board and inmates alike), Mr. T. L. Wright, Mr. Wright, jun., Miss Wright, Mr. W. Tomes, Mr. G. Vials, Mr. and Mrs. Gibbs, Mr. H. Law and the Misses

Cases were reported in the newspapers over the years of murder, suicide and abuse in the workhouse, not surprising as it housed a volatile mix of sad and desperate people confined together. The staff remained mainly unchanged over a twenty year period – they were unlikely to have had a pension and probably no savings so they had little option other than soldiering on to the end, even if frazzled and careworn themselves. Reading other accounts of good happenings at the workhouse it is hard to believe it is the same place – gifts and beer for the inmates on Christmas Day, outings, a visit to the Chrysanthemum Society on one occasion, it seemed idyllic! ***Workhouse at Christmas***

The inmates were desperate and in poor health and malnourished when they entered the workhouse, to be faced with long days of scrubbing, corn grinding, picking oakum (which was shredding the fibres of old tarred

192

rope) amongst other jobs. Soon their hands were not fit for other work even if they were to be offered it.

During the sixteen year period from 1889 there were 986 deaths, a few children, but surprisingly most who had reached their three score years and ten. From 1870 to 1906 there were 473 births in the workhouse, mostly illegitimate, around one in twenty was a stillbirth.

Those who were unmarried mothers had a really harsh existence. If they were not made to wear a yellow uniform, then they had a yellow stripe or badge on their dress to add to their shame and they were put to gruelling work in the laundry. At one time an allowance was made to unmarried mothers of 'a gallon for the bastard' this being an 8 lb or gallon loaf to keep the child for a week, supposedly if the child was too young to eat then the loaf was sold? In those days the saying 'it takes two' wasn't considered, it was the girl who took all the blame, regardless of the circumstances.

A man whose family ended up in the workhouse was punished severely –

Mount Gardens

William Wheeler a riveter of Mount Gardens was charged with deserting his wife and child, leaving them chargeable to Northampton Union 6th May 1882, their maintenance being 45 shillings. William had been away working, the case was adjourned for a week to allow payment, which with legal cost was £3.19 shillings. Did poor William ever get straight?

September 8th 1880 Thomas Partridge, also a riveter was charged with leaving his wife and four children chargeable to Northampton Union, expense incurred £135, not his first offence, sentenced to three months imprisonment with hard labour.

James Roberts a shoemaker was charged with leaving his child chargeable to Hardingstone Union to the cost of £14. James had entrusted the child to a woman to nurse, but she had taken it to the workhouse. The sentence was still one month's hard labour.

Yet another riveter, Thomas Daniels aged 32 of Liverpool, was charged with leaving his wife and three children chargeable to Northampton Union in August 1892, to the cost of £18.12 shillings, sentence six weeks hard labour.

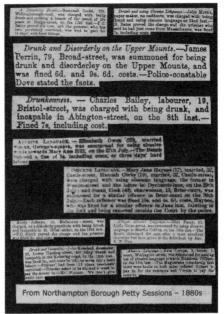

From Northampton Borough Petty Sessions – 1880s

Drink was the downfall of many. Newspapers were full of reports of court cases not only of men but women charged with being drunk and disorderly. The Market Square, Bridge Street and Wellingborough Road were often the scenes ..... not a lot has changed then!

Passages from Northampton Petty Sessions

Born the day before the 1881 census was Ada Green, daughter of Jane Green, charwoman aged 37. The informant on the birth certificate was Edward Abell master of the workhouse, the father's name is blank. Another unmarried mother on that census was Lucy Hoite aged 29, also a charwoman, born St Ives, Huntingdonshire. Her child was Jane one month old. Records show that Lucy also gave birth in the workhouse to a son Thomas 1875, and a male stillbirth in 1888.

Part of a birth certificate showing illegitimate status

Her family was difficult to trace due to the varied spellings of Hoite – Hoyte, Hight and Hite.

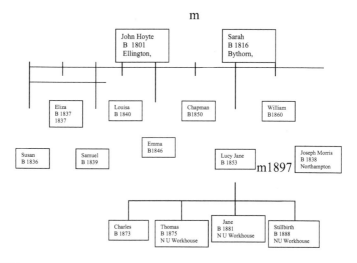

<u>1871</u>
John Hite was, living with son Samuel in St. Neots, a pauper.

<u>1881</u>
Lucy Hoite was in Northampton Union Workhouse.

Sarah Hoyt was at number 118 Kettering Road with her daughter Mary Miriam, who was married to James Brown, a shoemaker.

William Hoyte was at number 124 Kettering Road, a shoe riveter, married to Emma.

1891

Sarah Hoyte, a widow, was at number 29 Spencer Road with daughter Lucy, a laundress, and grandson Charles aged 18 a shoe pressman

1901

Lucy was living at number 20 St. James Street with Joseph Morris a labourer for the gas company, whom she married in 1897. Sarah Hoyt was still living with her daughter and by then aged 88.

..... and so it seems that much of the Hoite/Hite/Hoyt/Hoyte family left Huntingdonshire and came to Northampton.

Did Lucy at last find happiness and respectability and manage to stay out of the workhouse?

Sad that in past times the poor were so desperate to stay out of the workhouse and now in recent years the homeless have broken in for shelter. Vandals and the pigeons have done their worst, and the site is now an eyesore and a place of shame yet again for Northampton.

St.Edmund's Hospital / previously Northampton
Workhouse photographed 2008

Nazareth House, situated on the Barrack Road, described as 'Home for the Aged Poor and for Orphans', was another refuge for women who had fallen on hard times. Like the workhouse the women occupants were former domestic workers mainly. A house in Langham Place was used as a residence until the present Nazareth House was built in 1878.

How did so many from far away places end up in Northampton? Most it would seem were transferred from Nazareth Houses in other towns and cities, very few were from this town. The list of places where born reads like a gazetteer. The majority of both men and women were widowers and widows, and it is understandable how the older inmates came to be there. Many were in their 70s and 80s, too old and feeble to work. Surely it was a better existence than the workhouse.

But what of young adults?
1871 found Emma Parsons aged 5 living in Hackney with her parents Jane and Robert, and her brother Jacob aged 4, together with several lodgers. Ten years later, aged 15, Emma was living in Nazareth House, St Paul's, Hammersmith, listed as destitute in a House of Charity, alongside foundlings and orphans. Yet Emma's sister

two years older, her brother Jacob now aged 14, and a younger brother and sister were still living with the parents at number 19 Acton Street, Hackney. So why and how did a young girl such as Emma become the one who was homeless and destitute? A question that could have been asked in all the Nazareth houses.

The Sisters of Charity here in Northampton were also from far away, many from Ireland. Children's ages ranged from 5-16, the only boys were the under 5s, all listed as orphans and the majority from far away. They were taught in the institute, older girls were prepared for domestic service.

It is documented that orphans were sent to Canada from Nazareth Houses in Aberdeen, Oxford and Northampton sometime between the years 1869 and 1939. In Eastern Canada it is thought that 10% of the population is descended from orphan emigrants.

As well as those who came to the town to work, there were many who made the journey to start a new life elsewhere. There were those who emigrated, such brave people setting out on a long and arduous journey to the unknown.

'Lancashire Witch' sailed from East India Dock, London 2-7-1863 and arrived at Lyttleton, New Zealand 13-10-1863 a voyage of 107 days! Aboard was the Hight family who paid a deposit of £3, the balance of £7 and government aid was £24. Their ticket was number 458. Water and provisions were provided, with an extra quart of water while the ship was within the tropics. The cooking must have been most difficult, near impossible in such crowded unsavoury conditions ...... there were 202 emigrants aboard.

Henry Hight, 27, farm labourer
Elizabeth, 26
Albert, 4
Annie, 2
Mary Jane, 6 months

Also aboard 'Lancashire Witch' listed as from Northampton, but could have meant the county were:

Jesse Prestidge, 33, carpenter
Jane
6 children
plus Sarah Prestidge (sister), 28, domestic servant

There were 52 single women aboard who were granted free passage.

In 1851 Jesse (Joseph and Sarah Prestidge were living in Moreton Pinkney, aged 17 and 9, their mother Mary aged 44 was listed as pauper, husband transported. Could their journey to the other side of the world have been to find him?

There were 52 single women aboard who were granted free passage.

Another HIGHT who left these shores was Thomas Hight, a reaper, who was transported aboard the 'Asia 111' to Australia in 1825. His crime was entering an enclosure with a bludgeon with the intent to kill illegally. In 1819 Thomas had appeared before Rt Hon the Earl Spencer and sentenced to 12 months imprisonment for refusing to find surety for a misdemeanour.

Some others who emigrated from this town/county were found aboard the following:
'Fatima' sailed London to Port Adelaide 17-1-1850
Benjamin Hirrows, 34, shepherd
Mark Lines, 18, shepherd
John Wright, 28, labourer
Catherine(wife),23
    Child Elizabeth died at sea
Elizabeth Wright (sister), 27, domestic servant

'Constance' sailed from London via Plymouth to Adelaide 18-7-1850
Richard Andrews, 24, labourer/smith
William Buckley, 33, farm labourer
John Fairey, 33, farm labourer
Samuel Simpson, 27, farm labourer
William Tomkins, 26, shoemaker
Samuel Willis, 32, farm labourer
Jemima Willis, 24, domestic servant

'Eastern Empire' sailed from London to Lyttleton, New Zealand 28-8-1864
Thomas Jefcoate, 24, labourer
Janet J. Jefcoate, 25
Travelling with them were
Edward Ball, 31, Printer
Henry R Latchell. 17
James Palmer, 24

Also from Northampton were
James Brown, 25, farm labourer
John Helford, 21 farm labourer
Joseph Stratford, 22, farm labourer
Samuel Hight, 19, farm labourer
Rhoda Hight (sister), 17, domestic servant

In 1851 Samuel aged 6 and Rhoda aged 3 were living at High Street, Broughton with parents Samuel and Mary and five siblings. By 1861 Rhoda was working as a house servant for a farmer, John Mawby of Thorpe Malsor, and Samuel was still at home, an agricultural labourer. What made them decide to leave the family and undertake such a huge adventure?

These tales tell of just some of the places, people, problems and hardships that workers both arriving and leaving (willingly) encountered. If a great grandmother or other relative of yours was amongst them, be very proud because life was not easy for them. Many were the people without whom today's Northamptonians would not be here, they worked, they married, they stayed and became part of our heritage.

A Saunders 2007

Window of the Angel Hotel.

* Thanks given to Northampton Library

Coming soon

NORTHAMPTON HERITAGE HUNTERS

next publication

BY THE WAY TO KINGSTHORPE

The road to Kingsthorpe has been the scene of important national events, and the backdrop to scenes of everyday life. A ruined castle, heroes and villians, factories, fountains and graceful mansions can all be found along the way. In 1831, a local writer documented his favourite "stroll to Kingsthorpe by rural route". Victorian author George de Wilde retraced the journey thirty years later, amid the town's industrial expansion. Now Northampton Heritage Hunters follow his footsteps, and recount tales of people and places By the Way to Kingsthorpe.